FREEDOM'S REIN

The Autobiography of Shane Sellers

Shane Sellers
and
Tricia Psarreas

Freedom's Rein: The Autobiography of Shane Sellers depicts the events of Shane Sellers' life as he experienced them. The contents in this book are not intended to harm any of the people mentioned within these pages. This is a true story and the depicted events are not exaggerated or embellished. To learn more about the facts behind the story, please visit the book's official website.

Sellers, Shane and Psarreas, Tricia
Freedom's Rein: The Autobiography of Shane Sellers
First Edition

ISBN 978-0-9816040-0-8

Printed by King Printing in Lowell, Massachusetts, the United States of America

www.FreedomsRein.com

(800) 978-1505

Dedication

Shane Sellers would like to dedicate *Freedom's Rein* to
His beautiful wife Kelli and their three wonderful children
Shali, Saban, and Steiner.

Shane Sellers and Tricia Psarreas would also
like to dedicate this book to Barry Golden,
one of the kindest, most generous men they
have had the privelege of knowing.

"I would hurl words into this darkness and wait for an echo, and if an echo sounded, no matter how faintly, I would send other words to tell, to march, to fight, to create a sense of hunger for life that gnaws in us all."

Richard Wright
American Hunger
1977

FREEDOM'S REIN

The Autobiography of Shane Sellers

Prologue

Do you know what it's like for your body to cannibalize its own organs? For you to deprive your body of food for so long that it retaliates by eating itself?

I sincerely hope not.

But for many of the leading jockeys in the world, that feeling is all too familiar. In a sport where anything above two percent body fat is often considered "too fat" and 120 pounds is "too heavy," it's hard not to know that feeling.

Nowadays people are obsessed with the eating disorders that affect actors, singers, models, and the general public. Anorexia and bulimia have become household terms that practically make people shudder where they stand. Nobody likes the idea of an eating disorder and why should they? But when it comes to jockeys, eating disorders are allowed and almost expected.

In the horse racing world, every horse in every race has to carry a certain weight according to the "conditions" of that particular weight. That's the weight of the jockey and the saddle that must add up to a certain weight for a horse to lug around on a track. In theory, the differences in weight even up the competition. Better horses carry more weight which slows them down. Lesser horses carry less weight so they can run faster. Most people don't realize that different horses tote around more or less weight. But we jockeys sure know it.

If a jockey is under the weight assignment for a race, the weight can be raised by slipping thin slabs of lead into little pockets in the saddle. The total weight of the rider, the lead, and the saddle then lead to the correct amount of weight. But believe me, jockeys don't usually need extra weight; they need less.

The problem is that the weights are too low for modern times. How many grown men or women do you know who can make, say, 112 pounds to ride in a horse race? How about 122 pounds? In today's world, those weight limits are nearly impossible. But that's the way it is in horse racing. You want to ride thoroughbred horses at incredible speeds in famous horse races for thousands, or maybe even millions of dollars in prize money. On top of that, you have the chance to experience all the fame and glory and thrills that anyone could ever imagine. Well, if that's the case, then you'd better get rid of that weight – and you'd better do it in any way you can.

So we deprive ourselves of food, drink, and normal life as most people know it. We train all day, drink a bit of coffee, salivate over the food in the jock's room kitchen, and then retreat to the hot boxes where we can do nothing but sweat and think about the food that we really can't eat. If we do give into the temptation to bite into one of those juicy burgers, we know that the heaving bowl is right around the corner.

And man, do those heaving bowls get their use.

So we starve and we eat and we heave and we sweat. Then we try to control an animal that weighs about ten times more than we do. We struggle with our bodies as they go into starvation mode and we learn to deal with the dizziness, lack of energy, and literal stars that seem to be swarming around our field of vision. We tell ourselves that laxatives are as nutritious as those damn burgers that we can still smell while we starve and heave and sweat some more.

Then we mount our horses and put our lives at risk before every single race.

Now, I know what you're thinking. "Why do you do it? Why would you put yourself through that pain?" The answers to those questions are easy. You sacrifice. You sacrifice because you love the game that much.

Even with all I've been through – all the pain, embarrassment, and shame – I would be willing to sacrifice it all over again.

Why?

Because once you're in the game, the game is in you. It's in your blood, in your sweat, in your tears. It pervades your pores and takes over who you are and who you are to become.

You live it, you breathe it, you bask in it. And even when it bites you in the ass, you still love it as much as you did in the beginning.

As for me, I still can't get enough of it because I'm not just Shane Sellers, former jockey. I'm Shane Sellers, the horse racing industry's biggest fan.

Welcome to my world.

Part 1

Not-So-Sweet Home Louisiana

Chapter 1

Most kids run through their houses for fun. I used to run through my house to get away from the cockroaches.

My childhood home in Erath, Louisiana was the kind of place that you would see on a TV show that makes fun of rednecks. The house itself was tiny; so small that there was barely room to sleep. It consisted of a decent sized living room that led to a long kitchen. To the left of the kitchen was my parents' room. Through their room was the bedroom that I shared with my three siblings. Three boys and a girl, all living in one room.

It's not like it was a big room, either. My younger brother Ryan and I shared a bed, my older brother Keith had his own bed, and my little sister Kristy had her own bed. Cramming three beds into that tiny room didn't help things any. And with a 12 year age difference from my oldest brother Keith to my youngest sister Kristy, that situation was just plain weird as was the rest of our lives.

The second we would come from our room and turn the lights on, little bitty roaches would scatter around and run all over the house. They mostly stayed in the kitchen, creeping out of the cabinets, where they hoped to find a bit of food. The funny thing was that there really wasn't any food in my kitchen or anywhere else in my house for that matter.

My constantly rumbling stomach could testify to that fact.

To be fair, it's not that I was starving; I was just hungry for something different. All of us were. But even though we couldn't afford gourmet meals and we couldn't dine out at the best restaurants, my mother Glenda never let us go hungry. She was a great woman and she always took great care of us kids. We all respected her for that and we still do. She's the glue that's kept our family together and we love her for all she did.

My mom always had something for us to eat, even if it wasn't all that good. We spent many nights eating my not-so-favorite meal, rice and eggs. And that dish is exactly what it sounds like: white rice covered by two or three eggs from our chicken coop.

When I used to collect eggs from our chickens, sometimes I dreamed of bringing a chicken in the house and preparing the chicken to eat, instead. I imagined those breasts, wings, and thighs, just waiting for us to devour them. Then I imagined how hungry we would be if we chose one nice chicken meal over years of eggs, and sat down to eat my eggs and rice.

Of course, we loved meat and we ate it whenever we could. Sometimes we just didn't have a very practical way of getting that meat.

Some nights my dad would go poaching, also known as outlawing, to get us whatever kind of meat he could find. Since it was illegal to poach in Louisiana, the last thing he wanted was for the game wardens to hear his gunshots. Dudley Sellers had more than enough problems with our state's authorities as it was and there was no need to make matters any worse. So my dad's philosophy was to shoot something, grab it, stick it in the car, and get the hell out of there as quickly as possible.

He would creep around the local waterways robbing other people's crab traps, and sometimes he went poaching for geese. It wasn't easy for him to secure a whole family's worth of food illegally, but fortunately, being sneaky was the one thing my dad was really good at.

And in one of the few things we did together as a family, my father frequently brought along some of us kids for the illegal ride.

When you outlaw for food, you learn that animals know almost as much about securing meals as people do. For instance, rabbits head onto quiet roads to feed when it rains outside. And where the rabbits went, our hungry stomachs were sure to follow.

All the men in my family would pile into the station wagon and get ready to hunt. Granted, my dad was the only one who actually hunted, but he had no qualms about bringing me, my brothers, my uncle, and some of our cousins along for the ride. Not only did he lack qualms, but he made a game out of it. My dad would turn to my uncle with a big grin and say, "Hey Stanley, it's a good night. Come on, man, let's go kill some rabbits."

So that's exactly what we did.

Ever cautious of the game wardens, my uncle drove along the back roads, careful not to call attention to us. My dad sat in the passenger's seat with a gun between his legs, ready to make his move at any moment. As we drove along the rain slicked back roads, we watched for any rabbits that searched for their own dinners. Before the rest of us could even spot a rabbit, my dad was already on the move. With the car moving at 15 miles per hour, he would open his door, aim, and shoot. Then someone would throw the rabbit carcass into the back of the car and we would keep on going.

That's just the way it went. My dad would shoot a rabbit or two and throw them in the back of the beat up station wagon. Then my uncle would rush deeper into the back roads where my dad would shoot a couple more rabbits. Again, we would speed off. By the end of our trip, we could rush away from the back roads with 20 or 30 dead rabbits in the car.

The whole way home our hearts would pound. Not just for the thrill of the kill and not just because of the adrenaline rush we got from doing something wrong, but also because we knew that we would be able to eat the rabbits if we got away with our actions.

When we walked in my house with our hearts still pounding, we would get ready to skin, gut, and prepare the rabbits for dinner. The worst part of this process came when we opened up the rabbits. I've smelled a lot of things in my life and none of them are as rancid or foul as the smell of an open rabbit. I don't know what makes them smell as bad as they do, but when I was a kid, I didn't really care. All I cared about was that we were going to eat rabbit — and as repulsive as dead rabbits smell when they're gutted, they smell as delicious as they taste once they're cooked.

Looking back, I know that our methods of gathering food were wrong and more than a little unconventional. But as a kid, I didn't know any better. All I knew was that we were hungry and our dad could find us food when we didn't have another way to get it. That didn't make him my hero, but it *did* keep me from living off rice and eggs. Plus, I didn't actually do anything wrong, so it was easy to distance myself from the situation.

Sadly, the distance disappeared the day my dad made me take matters into my own hands.

One day my dad walked through our living room, past the bedrooms and the kitchen, and into our back yard — if it was big enough to really classify it as a yard. There he built his grandest invention: his very own butcher shop.

It wasn't really a butcher shop, but it might as well have been. He drove four wooden stakes into the ground and he attached chicken wire securely to the stakes to enclose the four sides. He tied the wire together tightly so nothing could get out from the sides. When he attached a screened lid to the top of the box, his invention was complete. The contraption was about six feet wide and ten feet long, the perfect size for the ultimate box of trickery. My dad threw a pile of rice chaff into the center of the box and propped up the screened lid with a long stick.

Captivated by the idea of a free meal, a bunch of blackbirds flew into the box to eat the alluring food that was available to them. What those blackbirds didn't realize is that we had a string attached to that stick, and that string was as good as any butcher's tool. My older brother Keith and I hid out by the box, waiting for some birds to take the bait. Once the rice chaff lured enough birds into the trap, we pounced. We pulled the string, dropping down the screened lid and trapping the blackbirds inside the box. And once we caught enough blackbirds that way, we got to work.

After we effectively trapped our prey in the box, Keith and I had to open the top of the box, careful not to let any of the blackbirds escape, so we could jump inside. We crawled around in the box, bumping into each other and into the walls. The birds flew around in a panic with their black wings in a fluster, pecking at our bodies, smashing into our heads, and doing anything they could to get out of what had been a bird's haven only moments before.

If you had been at my house as a spectator, I imagine this scene would have been quite a sight to see.

Keith and I swatted at the birds, grabbing onto them as quickly as we could. As they pecked and smashed and pecked some more, Keith and I just laughed at the sheer absurdity of our situation. Here we were, two poor kids, trapped in a box with a bunch of crazy birds – and as ludicrous as it was, we fully accepted our duty because our daddy told us to.

We knew that our situation was wrong and there were many things that we would have been happier doing at that time, but, we all pulled our weight in that house and we always came to terms with what we had to do – no matter how odd it was. And sometimes the best way to get through something crazy is to just smile and laugh your way through it. So that's exactly what we did.

Even as we twisted the birds' heads off and massacred every last one of them, we kept laughing because that was what we had to do to get ourselves through it. We knew our situation was bizarre, but that was the only lifestyle we knew.

However, we also knew enough to stop laughing once the hardest part of our job was done because in reality, there was really nothing funny about what we had to do.

Once we killed those 40 or 50 blackbirds, we crawled out of that box and kept our mouths shut. We had nothing to say to each other because there was really nothing that we could say. The only person we could talk to was my mom, so that's where I went.

I was already distressed over what Keith and I had just done, and the last thing I wanted to do was spend any more time with those feathery carcasses. I walked in the house and said, "Mom, we've got to go clean those damn blackbirds now. Why doesn't he get his ass out there and clean them himself?"

Ever the patient woman, my mom smiled a sympathetic smile at me and said, "Baby, you know how he is. There's nothing you can say about it, so just do it please."

I was going to do it anyway because I knew I had to, but I could never say no to anything my mama asked of me.

So heading back into the silence, I rejoined Keith in the yard and we tossed our soon-to-be dinner into a five gallon bucket. I don't think we made a sound as we threw the birds into boiling water for easier plucking and we stayed silent while we gutted the blackbirds and cut out their breasts. Then we continued to do our work quietly as we got rid of the legs, thighs, and everything else that was of no use to us because it was either too small or too gross to eat.

By the time we got to that point, there was really nothing left to say. We did what we had to do – what our dad *made* us do – and our work was done. The meat was ready and soon our mom would cook up the blackbird breasts with a bit of brown gravy and rice. We would eat and then we would never have to talk about it again.

But the problem with things that you think you'll never have to talk about again is that those are usually the things that usually haunt you the most.

During all this time of thwarting cockroaches, outlawing, and killing blackbirds, we had a family dog named King. Now I know that everyone says this about their dogs, but King was the best dog a family could ever hope for. He was a huge Doberman that looked like he could eat you whole, but in reality, King would never hurt anyone or anything. He was beautiful, he was faithful, and above all else, he was as loving as he was loved.

Unfortunately, some of us loved King more than others. I know that I would have given up some of my goose gumbo to keep King healthy, but my dad didn't agree. And when you're dealing with a macho man, a man's man, a kid's nightmare, there's nothing that you can do but go along with what the master says.

My dad owned us as much as he owned the dog, so the day that he said we couldn't afford to feed King any more was the day that we all had to say our mental goodbyes. Despite what anybody said and despite what anybody felt, my dad put his foot down. We couldn't waste any more of our food on a dog.

As days of hunger turned into weeks of starvation, we all watched as King withered away into nothing. His ribs started to show through his unhealthy looking coat and before we knew it, he was nothing but skin and bones. Our previously grand Doberman became a living skeleton. And even though we had the means to do something, we still couldn't save him.

Being the great dog that he was, King never lashed out at any of us or tried to leave. He never begged, he never whined, and he never let on to how miserable he was. Of course, we knew he was miserable. That was plainly visible. But still, King loved us as if we were the greatest owners in the world – a fact that makes this situation even more haunting.

One day King went inside his dog house and he never came back out. At that point, he was barely a dog anymore; he was nothing more than a fur covered skeleton. King was officially dead and we all knew that we could have saved him at any time.

As was usually the case with my dad, he didn't show any remorse. In fact, he didn't show any emotion at all. He just grumbled that we had to get rid of the body. And of course the 'we' that he referred to didn't include him. So we kids crawled into King's house and removed his corpse. Then we threw away what was left of our dog, our companion, and our best friend.

On that day, I think I threw away whatever might have been left of any respect I would ever have for my dad, too. But as time would tell, King was not the only thing that my father would destroy from the inside out.

Chapter 2

My dad never gave me a beating I didn't deserve. But the mental abuse? That's something that *no* kid deserves.

Growing up in the small town of Erath, I didn't have a chance to have a normal life. My father's reputation followed me – haunted me – wherever I went. People would look at me and say, "That's Dudley's boy." And the common assumption was that if you were Dudley's boy, then you couldn't be much different than Dudley himself.

The truth was that I was nothing like my dad when I was a kid. We only shared one thing in common: both of our fathers were very harsh on their sons.

My dad grew up with a very strict father who shaped who he would become, much like my dad shaped who my siblings and I are today. Though my grandfather was generally a great man, a hard working man, and the kind of man you would want to have with you in your lifeboat, he also had a mean streak. And that meanness really showed when it came to the way that he acted with my father.

My grandfather was a tough man and that meant my dad had to be tough, too. He did everything he could to make my father tougher and stronger, but his good intentions didn't work. Instead of becoming self-relying, my father just became angry. There were signs about the kind of man my dad was going to become; that there was something seriously wrong with him. But nobody ever took the signs seriously enough and my dad continued to get worse.

When he was a little boy, my father would go out in the yard and kill his parents' chickens. He would wrap his hands around their necks, snapping them like they were little twigs. For him, that was the best way to unleash his anger. When my grandfather caught him doing that, he beat him with a bridle, but that didn't help. My dad continued to kill chickens and torture small animals because that made him feel good in some sick way.

It was hard for my dad to escape his past, but he really didn't try too hard once he grew up. Just his appearance made him look like the malicious man that he was. He had a dominant, mean façade that made people want to back away from him. His face was always covered in a scowl or a frown or even an evil look that seemed to radiate from his eyes. Once you added his stocky, athletic body and the tattoos into the picture, people really didn't want to go anywhere near him – and those were just the people who didn't know him.

The people who knew my dad didn't need to take his appearance into consideration to know enough to stay away. He had a reputation as a street fighter, a hard ass, a womanizer, and a drunk, four terms that pretty much sum up who he was.

Instead of taking his miserable childhood and learning from it, he decided to pass the same kind of torture onto others.

When he grew up, my dad fought everybody that he could, just to prove that he was stronger, better. He fought in bars, on the streets, and anywhere else that he could stir up a bit of mayhem. The feeling of fists flying and knuckles connecting with solid flesh made him feel like more of a man. And since my dad had to be the epitome of a man, he fought as often as he could.

In fact, my dad fought so much that people eventually learned to stay away from him altogether. His violent reputation was well known and people knew about him as far as three or four towns away. Nobody wanted to go anywhere near Dudley Sellers, and for good reason. They figured that if they went near him, trouble would not be far behind. Knowing what I know about my father, I'm willing to wager that they were right.

Apparently his reputation didn't bother him because my dad never tried to be nice or good or normal. He always had to stand out from the crowd in the most negative way possible. Sadly, that behavior didn't just apply to the random men that he encountered; it also applied to the women he would eventually meet.

Unlike my dad, my mother is a wonderful example of what a parent – and a person in general – should be. Selfless, caring, compassionate, and loving, she is the sweetest woman you could ever hope to meet. She is a devoted wife, a loving mother, and a dear woman all around. She's the kind of woman who would take your pain if she could; the kind of woman who wants to see everyone happy.

But my dad didn't care. He still treated her like she was nothing – and that was even before they were married.

When my dad proposed to my mother, he didn't get down on one knee and tell her that he loved her and wanted to spend the rest of his life with her. He threatened her. My mother's dad didn't want her to get married; he wanted her to finish school. She didn't want to disappoint her father, but my father instilled fear in her heart. My mother was so afraid of his threats that she ran away and married him against her father's wishes.

There began my parents' marriage and my mother's Godly obligation to stay with her husband for better or worse. Unfortunately, it also sealed my mom's fate into a lifetime of abuse from the man who promised to love her and cherish her – the priest's words, not his.

Even when we kids were born, my dad didn't try to hide his behavior; he may have even flaunted it more. He would come home drunk at all hours of the night, yelling and screaming. My mom would try to keep him calm. She would tell him to keep it down just for us kids. But my dad didn't give a damn about his kids; at least he didn't care about our emotional well-being. Our house was tiny and you could hear everything from everywhere. He knew that, but he didn't care. So while the four of us sat quietly in our room, we would hear our dad yelling and hitting our mom.

I wanted to help her, to save her. All of us did. But as was the case with King, we had to keep our mouths shut. My dad did what he wanted to do and that's all there was to it. If we got involved, we would just make things worse.

So we kept quiet like we were supposed to and waited for the pounding to stop. The pounding of his fists, the pounding of our hearts, and the pounding of our consciences – we just wanted all of it to stop.

My dad wasn't ashamed of the way he treated my mom. I don't know how many times he said, "If Glenda ever tries to leave me, I have a bullet with her name on it." But I do know that he wasn't just talking amongst his friends when he said that; he said it to my mother's face. As bad as he was to her, as much as he hit her, she wouldn't leave. She stayed with her family because that is the kind of woman she was. Family was all we had and she wouldn't leave because she was in physical danger. So she stayed and he abused her even more.

Even when my dad wasn't physically abusing my mom, he was still a mental abuser. He loved women and for some reason or another, women seemed to love him back. My dad didn't care that his wife – the devoted woman who put up with his shit all day, everyday – was home waiting for him. He did whatever and whoever he wanted to do.

Case closed.

When he messed around on my mama, he didn't try to hide his actions. He paraded around with his other women right in front of us. Hell, sometimes he brought us along on his dates just for the fun of it. One time he brought Keith along with one of his girlfriends while they went out crabbing. My dad never thought about how that made Keith feel or about how awkward it probably made his date feel. He really did whatever he wanted.

On one occasion, my father stole Keith's shotgun and gave it to one of his girlfriend's sons. Keith loved that gun and it meant the world to him. He got it for Christmas and we didn't get many

Christmas gifts when we were kids. When Keith realized his gun was missing, he searched for it everywhere. He was going out of his mind trying to find out what happened to his present. When he finally discovered its whereabouts, Keith was devastated. It was as if our father chose another little boy to take Keith's place in the family. That experience bothered Keith so much that he still talks about it today.

But that's just how my dad was. He treated our mother like garbage and treated his girlfriends like royalty.

My dad's rendezvous' would have been embarrassing in any place, but they were especially bad in our town. Erath was a little bitty town where everyone knew each other's business. More importantly, Erath was a place where people loved to *talk* about each other's business. If you did something, the whole town could learn about it within minutes.

And man did my dad have a lot of gossip worthy actions.

It's not that the people of Erath were trying to be rude or stir up trouble; they simply had nothing better to do. Erath was a one horse town. When I was a kid, there were probably less than 2,000 people living there and they didn't have much to do with their time. They could go to one of the two small grocery stores, gossip with each other on the streets, or have some guests over for dinner.

But that's really how things were in Erath. People were simple back then; *life* was simple back then. We all lived in the same quietly-loud atmosphere and everything was always the same – until the town fair rolled around.

Once a year, our town put on a really enjoyable festival full of food, dancing, and all sorts of fun things. Everyone in Erath looked forward to this fair; especially us because that was the only fun time we had every year. We could run around like kids and have fun without any adults telling us what to do. The world was our oyster and we loved the fun and freedom that the town fair brought into our lives.

And even though we were excited by the idea of doing something fun and different, we *weren't* excited about everyone seeing our drunken dad strolling through the crowd with one of his random women in his arms.

How humiliating.

Every time I saw my father at the fair, I felt myself cringe. All I could concentrate on was my dad standing there with another woman on his arm while everyone we knew watched. My teachers were there, my friends were there, everyone was there. And everyone could see exactly what my dad was doing and why his nasty reputation was well earned.

That was horrible for me. It felt like the fair just stopped when we got there; like everyone's eyes were on us.

My siblings and I didn't have a fair shake. We were good kids. We were mischievous like anybody else, but we were good kids. Our dad helped make us that way and that's the one good thing he did. People didn't see it that way, though. Even my friends' parents would shake their heads while they watched my father stumble around drunk with another woman. A lot of people were looking down at me and I knew it. They knew I was poor, that I had nothing, that I was one of the kids that stood in the free lunch line. They knew that I was Dudley's son and they shunned me for it.

One of the few people who didn't look down on me was my fourth grade teacher, Nancy Toups. Mrs. Toups grew up with my father and she knew what he was like firsthand. Like the rest of the town, she knew about my dad's violence and drinking and womanizing. But unlike some people in the town, she didn't treat *me* badly because of it. In fact, she saw how hard I tried and always made me feel special.

Mrs. Toups knew how hard my dad was on me, particularly. She saw that my siblings were allowed to get Cs and Ds on their report card without having a problem, while I wasn't allowed to take home anything less than a B. She saw all of this – she saw everything – and she still didn't look down on me. Instead, she acted as an inspiration. Mrs. Toups always greeted me with a warm smile and she always had the nicest things to say. So when I saw her at the town fairs, I was embarrassed, but her warm look and gentle hug always made me feel like everything would be okay; that *I* would be okay. I suppose that's why she's one of the few people I will never forget because she gave me the little bit of self-esteem I had.

Unfortunately, a lot of the people of Erath didn't share my teacher's kindness and understanding. They saw what they wanted to see; they saw what they assumed was true. And rather than try to get to know me as an individual, they presumed that I was just like my dad; that I was the way my dad wanted me to be.

In their eyes, we were all equal. We were all nothing. We were nothing more than Dudley reincarnated. So they shunned us as much as they shunned my father and they assumed that they were doing the right thing.

With the way that my dad behaved, I don't know if I can blame them. But the thing is that I *wasn't* my dad. I had a heart of gold and I still do. That didn't matter, though. I had to suffer the stigma of being Dudley's son.

And that's probably the worst form of mental abuse a person can get.

Chapter 3

The true sign of a real asshole is when someone doesn't know or care how their actions make other people feel. If there's one thing I can tell you with certainty, it's that my dad was as big of an asshole as they come.

Of course, my father didn't see it that way when I was a kid and I don't think he sees it that way now. When I was younger, he wanted me to follow in his footsteps; to make him proud. But when you're talking about a man like him, it's impossible to ever be good enough to make him proud.

My dad wanted me to be like him and that's the way he tried to make me. I was a Chihuahua and he made me into a Pitbull. I had to fight the best; be the best. I had to be a fighter just like my father was. In a way, it's like he wanted to live his life all over again through me.

I would be outside playing in front of the house and my dad would come outside with the boxing gloves and throw them at me. Just like my grandfather did to him, he would sit there and watch while he made me fight with my friends. It didn't matter if there were two, three, or ten kids outside.

When my dad pulled out the gloves, I had to fight.

My dad didn't stop there, either. If I got a bad grade or did something to bother him, he threw the gloves at me and made me fight him. He would hit me and hit me until blood flowed from my nose. If I didn't hit him back, he would hit me even harder. The situation was terrible and I wanted nothing more than to escape.

Even if I tried to run it wouldn't have done any good, though. Dudley's son wasn't allowed to run from a fight. The very idea of trying to avoid a fight was fearful. So I fought out of fear of getting my ass whipped. And since I had to fight, I eventually learned to win.

He didn't have the words to say it, but that made my dad proud. When it all came down to it, he wanted me to be just like him.

But in order to be like him, I had to be more than a fighter. I had to be an athlete. My father was a very talented athlete when he was younger. In school, he earned the nickname 'The Flying Frenchman' because he could run so fast. He was the first man in Louisiana to ever run the 100-yard dash in under ten seconds flat, and that's a mighty big record. My father also used to play football and box when he was younger. Since he couldn't do any of those things anymore because of his age or his drinking or both, he made it a point to make sure that I could.

My running days began soon after we moved to Erath from a trailer in Lockport, Louisiana. The day my father first saw me run must have also been the day that he decided to make me his prodigy. He saw talent in me and he made sure to make that talent soar. He didn't encourage me the way most parents would. Instead, he made me regret the day I ever showed him how fast I was.

Once my dad saw what I was capable of, he worked me to the bone. While other kids were outside playing in their yards, I was at the track running 50-yard dashes. My father held onto his stopwatch and always reminded me that I couldn't cheat the clock. So my dad rode me hard and pushed me for everything I had. I always had to run harder, faster, better. Harder, faster, better.

Just like with fighting, I had to become the best.

When I ran, my dad used to always tell me that I had talent, that I had stamina. When I heard him say that, it pumped me up. I wanted to please my dad more than anything; I wanted him to be proud of me. As rotten as he was, I couldn't help but crave his approval. I wanted him to love me like a father should love a son. Every once in a while he showed his love, but those moments did not come often. That's why I got so excited when he talked about my talent; it meant that he accepted me on some level. He couldn't show me his pride, though. All of his compliments were always countered by insults. I could have broken every track record in the book and it wouldn't have mattered. I could never be good enough.

My dad didn't see our running and fighting sessions as torture; he saw them as bonding. He wanted me to be a miniature version of him and that's what he trained me to become. When he was a kid, he boxed, ran, and played football, so he thought I should do the same. I had the talent and drive that he had as a kid, but I had one thing that he didn't: I had heart. My dad wanted to see what he could have done with his life if he chose to do it, but he just didn't have the heart to make something better of himself.

That's one of the things that hurts and annoys me the most about my father: he never wanted to try.

He used to work in the oil field, but he hurt his back and became disabled. If you ask me, that was nothing more than an excuse. A man who can crawl along levies to catch geese and throw all sorts of carcasses into the car can do *some* kind of work. He could have gotten a desk job. He could have done *something*.

Instead, he stayed out drinking from the night before and we watched my mama walk miles and miles to work so that she could provide for our family. He secured food in any way that he could so that he could drink away my mother's hard earned money.

Then he sat back and made me run some more.

And even though I was running for him, it felt like I was running away from him. While my muscles pumped and my pores leaked sweat, I let my mind take me to a different place. I had no particular place in mind; just a place that wasn't *there*. So I ran and ran, all the while wishing that I was somewhere else.

If I started to slack, my dad would get on my case. He made sure that I had more to worry about than him being angry; I had to worry that *God* would be angry.

My dad didn't do much for me along the line of principles and values, but he did teach me to fear God. He threatened me with God like a parent threatens a child that Santa won't come this year if the kid misbehaves. After all, I couldn't fool God any more than I could fool a stopwatch – and those *are* my father's words.

But the truth of the matter is that I wouldn't have fooled God if I could have. Despite everything that I went through during my childhood, I always believed that God was watching me; that He was looking after me. In a way, God was the kind and loving father that I didn't have at home.

So even though my family stayed home on Sunday mornings, I always made it a point to go to church. Our church was only two or three blocks away from my house, so I walked there every Sunday. Since none of my friends went to church unless their families made them go, I usually walked alone.

I could feel my heart beat a little bit faster as I approached the grand church that almost looked out of place in our town. Erath wasn't in shambles, but it wasn't exactly nice, either. This church was absolutely beautiful and it was hard to believe that this building was in the same area – or even the same world – as our little town with two grocery stores and one red light.

I spent about five years as an altar boy and I loved every minute of it. I would walk in the back door to the altar boy's corridor and all of my troubles seemed to melt away. Father Armante would smile his infamous smile at me and I was at peace with myself, with my family, and with the world. Still feeling wonderful, I got to work with the other altar boys, preparing holy bread for mass.

During mass, I would listen to Father Armante speak about God and his words lifted my heart. While I was in church, I felt like nothing else mattered; like everything would be okay. I had no more negative feelings about my life because I was so consumed with my inner peace and my surroundings. All that existed was the sweet smell of incense, Father Armante's gentle voice, and the feeling of God in my heart. It was a very spiritual feeling and I felt like I was in Heaven.

The Catholic Church gave me everything that I was missing in my home life. It was somewhere that I could be at peace; it was something that I needed. I felt great while I was there and I felt just as great when I left. When I walked home, I didn't let my living conditions bother me. I didn't think of my dad and his boxing gloves, or the sounds of him abusing my mother, or the women that he ran to when he left my mama at home.

It didn't matter that I was walking back towards Hell because God was on my side.

And even with all of the things that would eventually come, God would always be there, right where I needed Him and when I needed Him the most.

I just wish I could say the same for some of the other figures that have drifted in and out of my life.

Chapter 4

My life didn't really start until I moved to Erath, but there is one phenomenal event that happened before I made the big move from Lockport, Louisiana. My family and I didn't travel often, but we did go on one trip that would change my life forever. In fact, it would *make* my life forever.

While we still lived in the trailer in Lockport, we went to visit my grandmother in Erath. It was Christmastime and I knew what that meant: good food, a few presents, and the feeling of love that radiated from my grandmother, my aunts, and my cousins. What I didn't expect was that the ride to Erath would shape the rest of my life and who I was to become.

Along our drive, we saw a lot of things that you would expect to see on the way to Erath: small towns, undeveloped oil fields, and a whole lot of shrubs. Then without warning, the scenery changed.

There were horses ahead!

I sat on my knees with my hands on the window, staring at the horses like they were God's answer to my prayers. I didn't know what it was about those horses that captivated me so much, but I knew that I was hooked. It was just a feeling; an instinct. I had a newfound passion for horses and I suddenly knew I needed to be with them.

The whole time we were in Erath, all I wanted to do was spend time with the horses. Something about those horses called out to me and I had never been as interested in anything before in my life. I wanted to learn as much as I could about them. Not horse racing; just horses. At that time, I didn't even know what horse racing was. And if you had told me, I don't think I would have even cared. I was just interested in the horses and nothing but.

And those horses gave me plenty of reasons to be interested. They were magnificent; they were mesmerizing. I couldn't get enough of the colorful splashes of brown, white, and black that covered the most enormous and beautiful animals I had ever seen. Even more impressive than their physical appearance was their mentality. Those horses were smart and they seemed like they knew it. Basically, those horses were everything that a creature should be.

Before then, I had only seen horses from watching Cowboy and Indian movies. I loved watching those movies and those were one of the few things I could ever watch with my dad without having any problems. We had one TV in the living room and as was the case with everything else, he was in control of the programming. If you didn't like what he was watching, your only option was to leave the room. But when a Western played, I could sit there and watch to my heart's content.

I loved to see the horses and he loved to see the Westerns. When one of those Cowboy and Indian movies came on, I was really excited for two reasons. First, I could watch what I wanted to watch. Second, I could have a rare bonding session with my dad. Our bonding sessions were few and far between, so movie nights were one of the few highlights of my childhood.

Strangely, when I watched those movies, I never cared for the cowboys that rode those horses. In fact, I thought something about them was just plain mean. I may have been a kid, but I didn't understand why those cowboys wanted to swoop in on their steeds and steal the Indians' land. Really, I thought about that! So when we played Cowboys and Indians, I always wanted to be an Indian.

But when it came to those old Westerns, I just wanted to see the horses.

When we packed up our belongings and moved to Erath, I was thrilled that horses could very possibly become a big part of my life. Other than my weekly visits to church, my involvement with horses was the single thing that really kept me going.

Pretty soon after I moved, I got my first taste of a life away from my family. When I went out in Erath, I never wanted my brother Ryan tagging along any more than my brother Keith wanted me to tail him. Three year age gaps between brothers seem astronomical when you're a kid, so we were all content to make our own friends and save our family time for the house when we needed each other the most.

So I made it a mission to make some friends and it didn't take me very long. I met some kids from down the road who had race horses. That was like a dream come true to me. I had friends to play with – *and* horses to see. My friends were great, too. We always wanted to get together and sleep at someone else's house, running the streets like kids. So we played with the horses, we played with each other, and we had a great time all the while. At that age, nothing could have been better – or so I thought.

When I was 11 years old and I had already experienced all the horrors of living with my dad, I had another rare father-son bonding moment with him. We were watching the Kentucky Derby together on television and I felt more captivated by the horses than I ever had before. I was sitting in Indian style on the floor, but I was thinking more like a Cowboy when I turned to him and said, "I want to do that."

My dad looked at me with interest and said, "Oh yeah?" He sat there for a moment thinking it over and then he said, "I'm going to find somebody to help you do that then."

And wouldn't you know it, that's exactly what he did.

My dad hooked me up with an old man named Mr. B.B. Hebert so I could learn everything there was to learn about horse racing. When I was still 11 years old, I spent the summer in Abbeville, about five miles from Erath, with Mr. B.B. and I think I learned more during those few months than I learned throughout the entire school year.

Mr. B.B. lived across the street from his brother, Clement, who was the owner of Hebert's Meat Market. The market was directly across the street from the 'bush track.' That was the perfect place for me to learn about horses because I wasn't just hearing about it; I was living it and breathing it from sunrise until sunset. I'll never forget the sound of the roosters out back crowing and the smell of horse feed, hay, and shit.

It might not sound so great, but I was in all my glory.

During that summer, I became really good friends with Mr. B,B.'s son Darryl. He shared his bed with me while I was there and his dad would come in every day at 5:00 in the morning to wake us up. Darryl moaned and groaned and promptly fell back asleep the first five or six times his dad came in his room. Me? I was up and ready to go. I couldn't wait to get up and start my day.

At the beginning of every day, I gave the horses baths and cleaned their stalls. I worked with a lot of older people, hard working people, the best people in the world. Once the horses were fed, and the stalls and farm were clean, I got to jump in the tractor to move on to the next task of the day. I drove the tractor around while the other guys gathered up dried corn stocks and threw them in the back. Once we collected enough, I would drive the tractor back so we could grind everything up and make chicken feed.

At some point we would go inside to eat breakfast, but then we went right back to work. And even though the work was hard, it still felt more like play than anything else. This wasn't cleaning blackbird guts; this was having a good time being around the horses and the farm.

Once we were finished with our chores, I finally reached the pinnacle of my day. The work was over and it was time to have some real fun.

Mr. B.B. would get on his 22-year-old pony named So Stand and put me on a race horse. At that time, I remember those horses feeling like Mac trucks. Those horses were huge, but I wasn't intimidated. My dad raised me not to fear anything and to jump headfirst into everything that I did. So that's exactly what I did when it came to the race horses.

Of course, I was young, so I couldn't do all that much by myself. Mr. B.B. would pony next to me on his horse and teach me how to ride. I sat on my little saddle with my knees pulled up while he sat on his full saddle and controlled my horse. His lead shank attached to my horse's bridle so he could keep it from doing anything crazy while I was on it. At that point, I was *far* from being a professional jockey, so we had to take things slowly.

Thus Mr. B.B. would pony me around his property, going round and round his small track at a slow gallop. I got a feel for the horse and for racing on a slow scale. It was going to take some time, but Mr. B.B. would teach me everything I needed to know: balance.

Mr. B.B. was sort of like the father figure who holds onto the back of a bicycle to make sure that his kid doesn't fall off. Once the kid can ride himself, his daddy can let go and get rid of the training wheels.

And that's what Mr. B.B. was to me when I started riding – he was my metaphorical set of training wheels. He was like a dad and he was very proud of me.

Everything about that summer was amazing. I loved getting away from my house and staying with Mr. B.B. and his family. It was a stable home and aside from being with horses, that was what I wanted more than anything else.

If there's one thing I'm thankful for about my dad, it's that he set me up with Mr. B.B. He found someone who could be proud of my accomplishments and who couldn't believe that an 11-year-old kid wanted something so badly. Mr. B.B. put me to the test everyday and I passed every test with flying colors.

My first really *big* test came about halfway through the summer when something amazing happened: I got my first real taste of the 'bush track.'

To make a long story short, a bush track is a small, unsanctioned, informal race track. Most bush tracks are located in rural areas where the authorities don't mind people having a bit of fun. That was certainly the case at Clement's track in Abbeville.

Louisiana is noted for producing some of the best jockeys in the world, and that is largely because these jockeys got a head start at this very track. By the time they were old enough to ride at recognized tracks, they already had a huge advantage. They'd spent years racing and preparing on our informal bush track, ridden hundreds of races where all kinds of things could – and did – happen. So they knew what most young jockeys couldn't hope to know yet: balance, breaking through the gates, and competition.

This little bitty track may not have seemed like much. The spectators stood up to watch the races. There wasn't a swank Turf Club, no manicured paddock with swaying palm trees – and no million-dollar thoroughbred racehorses. Just horses with no pedigree that we raised down there in Louisiana. A lot of the jockeys were only 12 or 13 years old, but they rode their horses like hell-afire. It was the perfect training ground for the kids who would eventually become many of the world's greatest jockeys.

Clement's was also the perfect atmosphere for a kid who wanted to see the good and fun of horse racing, rather than just focus on the thrill of being in a race. At our bush track, the races weren't the only events we looked forward to. We were excited about everything that happened before, during, and after every race.

On Friday nights, the Cajuns gathered together at Clement's to match their horses and see who would compete on the coming Sunday, drink themselves silly, talk shit about each other's horses and their odds of winning (or losing), and lay down the rules for the upcoming Sunday's races. Sometimes they would get so involved that they would outline the conditions for the next two or three weeks' races. No matter what they actually planned for, the point is that they had a great time doing it.

Cajuns, who make up most of the population of Southwest Louisiana, down near the Gulf of Mexico around Erath and Abbeville, are known for a lot of things, including a 'Joie de Vivre' lifestyle – which means they live a 'life of fun.' Cajuns work hard, but they play even harder. They have a great time whenever they can and the races were one of the places where they could certainly cut loose and have a great time.

At Clement's track, the races were always a lot of fun. The races weren't that long, but they didn't have to be. The track was straight and it was about three furlongs long, which is three-eighths of a mile or a little under 700 yards. The races usually matched two horses, going head-to-head. But sometimes we would make it a "heat" and have as many as four or five horses in the race. Famous big-time racetracks like Santa Anita or Saratoga or Churchill Downs are oval-shaped, and generally a mile or more around, with wide, sweeping turns able accommodate at least 12 horses, and sometimes as many as 20 at a time, like in the Kentucky Derby. Clement's was just a narrow straightaway, but that was all the track we needed.

The races began at a starting gate that was similar to a traditional starting gate, but it was much cruder. Once the horses were all loaded and in position, someone pulled a rope to open the doors. Then the jockeys yelled as loudly as they could to make their horses charge out of the gates. The sound of jockeys hollering scared the daylights out of the horses and made them run like hell. Before you knew it, these horses were off and the race was on.

So even though the bush track was not nearly as grand as a professional racetrack, the excitement in the air was still the same.

Throughout the day, people gathered in a small building right next to the track where they could seek refuge from inclement weather, or they could buy hot dogs, hamburgers, or mostly beer. Then everyone would head down to the track and get ready to watch the race and see who would put their money where their mouths had been the night or week or month before.

Well, halfway through that summer I found out that I was going to get my first opportunity to do more than stand on the sidelines. I wasn't just going to *watch* the jockeys ride; I was going to *be* one of those jockeys.

My daddy's uncle had a horse named Good Time Susan and he wanted to let me ride on the 'bush track.' In his old Cajun accent, my uncle turned to my dad and said, "I'm gonna give him a chance, Dud. I'm gonna put him on Sunshine Susan."

I couldn't believe my luck. That was the moment that my whole summer built up to and I couldn't wait to be in my first real race.

Mr. B.B. didn't want me to ride, though. He didn't think that I was ready. I know I was only 11 years old and that I weighed 62 pounds, but I wanted to do this; I needed to do this. I didn't want to wait until the end of the summer like Mr. B.B. told me to do. I wanted to ride right then.

So I ignored Mr. B.B.'s advice and I headed down to Clement's with my helmet and all my gear. My uncle was ready to put me on his horse, so I went over there more excited than I can ever remember being.

Then the worst thing that could have possibly happened to an 11-year-old kid happened. At the last minute, my uncle decided that he didn't want me to ride his horse. He was going to put Kim 'Kimbo' Frederick on, instead. He took me off before I even got a chance to ride and I was devastated.

I cried and I cried, and suddenly I was surrounded by a security net like I had never experienced before.

Mr. BB was mad.

My dad was furious.

My daddy went down there yelling and screaming at my uncle, so angry that I thought he was going to hit him. I know he wanted to, but he didn't. Instead, my dad yelled and yelled about how he couldn't believe that my uncle would do this to me after I put so much work into this opportunity; that I *wanted* this opportunity so badly.

For the first time in my life, my dad felt really bad for me and he wanted to help make me feel better; he wanted to make me happy. So he bought me a Shetland pony.

It didn't make up for all the years of hurt, but it sure did help.

Chapter 5

When my dad bought me a pony, he did two things: he cheered me up and he brought me closer to my buddy Dale Reaux.

His mom, Miss Donna, treated me like her own. I think I spent more time at their house than at mine. If Dale got yelled at, so did I. If Dale got whipped, so did I. We did everything together and we were treated like brothers.

Now that Dale and I both had ponies, we made it a point to ride together everyday. We made our own races under very simple terms. Then we hopped on our Shetlands' backs and got ready to have the time of our lives.

During that period, almost every day was the time of our lives. We talked and raced and laughed for as long as we could. I spent almost all of my spare time with Dale, racing our ponies until they couldn't race anymore.

Then one day when Dale and I woke up, we noticed something strange. The night before there were only two ponies.

Now there were suddenly three.

My little black pony was there, Dale's pony was there, and there was a little brown pony there, too. I never knew my Shetland was pregnant. That was the last thing I expected! That was the last thing *anyone* expected – except maybe for my pony.

I would have never ridden my pony if I knew that she was pregnant and about to give birth to a foal.

Dale and I laughed and laughed, and then there was only one thing I could say to the new Shetland.

"Sorry I beat so hard on your mama yesterday."

And with that, we had a new member of the family. I kept that baby in the backyard of our house and raised it as best as I could. My yard was twice as big as my house, but that's not saying much. It definitely wasn't big enough to raise a horse, but I didn't care. I had a new pony and I wasn't going to get rid of it – even if it was an unexpected addition to the family.

During that time, I was still upset about getting pulled off my first mount in a horse race, but it turned out that there was nothing to be too upset about. I had two ponies, I gained a bit of experience, and I was having the time of my life.

Then at about the same time that my surprise pony was born, my friend Nathan Granger had his daddy put me on a horse. That was the first horse I ever rode in a race and this horse was the real thing. He was a top triple A quarter horse, so he sure could run – and that was something that my pony didn't prepare me for.

Up until then, I only broke out of the gates a couple of times on the old 22-year-old pony So Stand. I was very inexperienced and I was also very small. In order to meet the conditions for the race, I had to put on a saddle with 20 pounds of lead. I only weighed 62 pounds and nobody would be happy if I won the race because I had a 20 pound advantage over the next jockey. So I had to compensate for my small size by adding more weight to the saddle.

Once I saddled up, I knew I was on a real horse for a real race. My whole family was there, waiting to cheer me on and support me no matter how the race went. I could see my mother's proud face, my father's drunken expression, and the rest of my family's anticipation that shone through their faces. My grandparents had never seen a race before, so they may have been more excited than anyone. I was excited, but more than a little terrified.

As scared as I was, I wasn't going to back down. I wasn't raised that way. So I listened to the voices around me and tried to remember everybody's advice and comments.

"You're not ready to use a whip, so just hold his head up."

"You only have to go 350 yards."

"Get to gate five so the race can begin."

"Don't stop until you reach the pole past the finish line."

Everybody had a lot of things to tell me, but the one thing that I heard over and over again was that I'd better holler. After all, I didn't have a whip and I needed some way to make the horse run as fast as its competitor.

So I kept everyone's advice in mind, headed over to gate five, and waited for my cue. Then the race was on.

When the gate opened, I was trying to hold his head up while I held on for dear life. I hollered louder than any boy has ever hollered before. All of a sudden, the horse was whooshing and I was whoa-ing. This thing was flying. All I could think about was how fast the horse was going and all I could feel was the rush of wind towards my face. I had never gone that fast on a horse and I was instantly hooked. I wasn't scared anymore. It was a rush.

While I continued to hold on and holler, it suddenly struck me that everyone else around me was hollering, too. I won the race by two or three horse lengths and my first real race was the first – and possibly the most important – victory of my lifetime.

I'll never forget the excitement on everyone's faces while they congratulated me and applauded. Everybody was really happy for me, especially since they all saw my disappointment when my uncle pulled me out of that race earlier in the summer. My friends patted me on the back and my family had plenty of hugs to give me. My mother exclaimed, "I knew you could do it!" while Mr. B.B. smiled and said "That's my boy." Everyone was happy for me and I was just as happy for myself.

Even though my dad came straight to the races from drinking the night before, I knew he was proud of me. And I was grateful that he found Mr. B.B. for me to give the best opportunity of my lifetime.

That moment was the highlight of my whole summer. I still raced whenever time and circumstances allowed it and I won my first 11 races. Each win was just as exciting as the next and I was convinced that this was what I wanted to do with my life.

When the summer was over, I went back home, but I still visited Mr. B.B. and Darryl as often as I could. I also started to stay with Dale a lot more frequently. That was like my second home. I was now riding their horses. Dale's dad Mr. Stanley saw something in me. Because of him, other people began to use me. He was the best gateman around and he taught me how to leave the gates. He taught us *all*.

Once the school year started back up, I had to get back to my regular life. I started playing football again because that was my dad's favorite sport. So I balanced my time between doing my homework, staying at Dale's, being with horses, and playing a bit of football and baseball with my good buddy Kenny Desormeaux. On Sundays I went to church and then to the match races. As the summertime faded, I was back to my normal, albeit improved, life.

And then my life threw another curveball at me just for good measure.

I was playing in a peewee league football game and my whole family was there to watch me. I was 13 years old and only weighed 75 pounds, but I still played middle linebacker. Outside of riding, football was my life. Unfortunately, my size was never going to allow me to get very far in my second favorite hobby.

During one of the plays, the fullback ran right through the line, coming straight at me. As I lowered to tackle him, we hit each other head-on. I made the tackle and we both hit the ground. He got up, but I didn't.

Suddenly, I felt a shock from my neck to the tip of my toes. With a hard thud, I landed on my back, almost certain that I just broke my neck; that I was paralyzed; that everything was over.

With a hit like that, I thought that had to be the case.

I lied there like that for what felt like a lifetime and when I looked up, my dad was standing over me. He put his hand on me and asked if I was all right. I immediately went into defense mode like he taught me to. I tried to shrug it off as if nothing had happened and I used my macho voice to say that I was fine and I could play. I lied through my teeth and said, "Just put me back in the game, dad. I'm alright."

But that day, my dad didn't want to see the act he taught; he truly wanted me to be okay. Since I clearly wasn't okay, my dad told the coach to pull me out of the game, so that's what the coach did. My dad took me back home and willingly let me quit the first thing I had ever quit in my life.

When we got home, I was afraid that my father was going to be angry; that maybe his concern was just an act, too. As it turned out, that wasn't the case. For the first time ever, my dad sat me down and spoke like a father to his son.

He used a kind voice as he said to me, "Let me tell you something. If you had the body to do it, you could be as good of a football player as you want to be. But your heart is just bigger than your body."

Surprisingly, his speech didn't end there. My dad looked at me honestly, maybe even lovingly, and continued on to say, "Now you need to make a choice. You need to think about what's best for you and your body. You need to ride horses or you need to play football. You can't do both and I can't make the choice for you."

Something about my dad's words made me reevaluate my life. I don't know if it was his kind words or his decision to let me choose or the love that seemed to be radiating from his eyes. Maybe it was all of those things. Maybe it was something else entirely. Whatever it was, my dad's speech made me realize that I did have to make a choice and that I wanted it to be the right one.

And you guessed it; horse racing won by a landslide.

So I stopped playing football, I stopped playing baseball, and I stopped doing everything else that couldn't advance my horse racing skills – my eventual horse racing career. I just focused on what mattered the most to me and put my whole heart into horse racing.

That's where I belonged and I knew it.

But alas, the road to getting where you belong is not always an easy one. That's why not many 12-year-olds have steady jobs.

When luck was against me, I was pulled out of a few more races. I suddenly questioned my ability to ride and wondered about the things I gave up for the sake of the game. Would I have been more successful at football? Could I ever be a jockey if I kept getting pulled off of horses? I didn't know.

But for the first time in my whole life, I was so discouraged that I thought of doing the unthinkable. I thought of quitting.

Then one day Dale's dad Stanley came to pay me a visit. He gave me an interested look and asked, "What are you doing?"

I nonchalantly answered, "Just playing."

He raised an eyebrow and said, "Where's your saddle? Miss Dunnbud's in this weekend and you're riding her."

When I heard Stanley talk about that horse, I didn't even want to respond. So I summoned up my weakest voice and said, "But I quit."

Then Stanley responded with a voice that was the very opposite of weak and said, "You're not quitting and you're never going to quit again. You never quit nothing and you're not a quitter." Still speaking strongly, Stanley said, "Now go grab your tack. We're breezing her today and you're going to ride her this weekend."

At the time, I didn't want to listen to him, but I knew I had to do something. So I grabbed my things and I did what Stanley told me to do. I rode Miss Dunnbud and I won. I literally got back on the horse and picked up where I had left off. And then without warning, the rush came back.

I was back where I belonged and there was nothing that could ever make me leave again.

Well, almost nothing.

Chapter 6

Like I said, Louisiana is home to many of the world's leading riders. What you might not realize is that I learned and raced with the best of them long before the world knew who these people were.

I rode with a lot of people when I was a kid, one of whom was Calvin Borel.

In 2007, Calvin won the Kentucky Derby. In 1977, Calvin and I hung around and rode horses together at Clement's.

When we were 12 years old, Calvin and I started riding together and we kept riding together for the next four years until we were old enough to ride at the recognized tracks. Whenever we could, we just rode and rode, talked and talked, played and played. We were great friends; we were like brothers.

Calvin is one of the most respectable horsemen I have ever been around as a child or as an adult. I always felt that if I couldn't win a big race, Calvin is the person I would like to see have that honor.

He's really that good of a guy.

No one has problems with Calvin and there's no reason why they should. Calvin has always been a hard worker, a great friend, and a fantastic guy all around. He never starts trouble with anybody and he's well respected because of that.

Calvin's parents had a huge litter of kids and Calvin was the last of the bunch. To this day, all of Calvin's friends call him Boo

Boo because that's what he was; he wasn't supposed to happen. Once he was born, though, he became everyone's favorite mistake.

Calvin was really close to everyone in his family, but he was closest to his older brother Cecil, a former jockey. Eventually, Cecil took Calvin in and played the roles of a racing mentor and a sort of father figure in his life. Calvin worked with Cecil from sunup until sundown. Sometimes they worked together for even longer than that.

Cecil was a great horseman and he taught his brother everything he knew. As Cecil taught Calvin to ride, he made sure that Calvin could get on the rail and stay on the rail like nobody else. He etched it into his mind.

If Cecil saw Calvin stray away from the rail, he would punish Calvin the next day by making him walk the horses with a shank rather than galloping horses. Cecil would say, "Just keep walking around the shedrow until you learn how to turn left." And even though that was supposed to be a punishment, it was one of the greatest things Cecil could have done for Calvin as a rider.

So Calvin always rode the rail like nobody else, even when he was just a bug boy. I suppose that's why he's known as one of the best 'rail riders' today. He's such a great rail rider that people eventually started calling him Calvin Bo-Rail.

By the time Cecil took Calvin in and trained him even more intensely, Calvin knew almost everything he needed to know about horse racing. His work ethic was incredible and he pushed himself as far and as hard as he could. Cecil taught Calvin a lot and that knowledge certainly paid off over the years.

Of course, Calvin and I did some horse racing research of our own. Every Friday night we went down to the bush track where they held a supper. That's where everyone would eat, drink, and match their horses. They laid down the conditions of the races and got as drunk as they could in the process.

Calvin and I would spend most of the night playing pool and waiting to see what was in store for us. Once everyone wrote down their conditions and plans on the chalkboard, we went over to see what we should expect. Then we knew who was racing which horse in what race and we could say, "I'm riding this one and you're riding that one."

We couldn't wait to see what was going on with those races because on Sunday we would be able to ride.

Most of these races were small match races, but we had a few bigger ones, too. I usually raced with Calvin and Kimbo Frederick, but every once in a while, we would find ourselves surrounded by what felt like celebrities.

Of course, they weren't really celebrities. They were local jockeys just like us who had already made a name for themselves on the recognized racetracks. We didn't see it that way at the time, though. To us, these jockeys were better than rock stars because for the most part, these jockeys didn't come back to Abbeville just because they wanted to ride on the bush track again.

Cajuns had a big role in everything that happened in the Louisiana racing world. They made bets on some of the most absurd things and they weren't afraid to spend a fortune to see who would win a bet.

I've said it before and I'll say it again: Cajuns work hard and play even harder.

The Cajuns placed bets on some of the strangest things that would make an outsider scratch his head in wonder. Sometimes they would put a girth on the horse and tie empty beer cans with rocks in them to the horse's back. Then they would race two horses against each other with no jockeys. Which spooked horse would win? Only the race could tell.

And those were the kind of races that stand out in my mind more than any others. I remember one particular occasion when some of the local Cajuns brought Ronnie Ebanks and Randy Romero to Clement's for what must have been one of the craziest races in history. Both of those jockeys rode at recognized racetracks, so Calvin and I were shocked to see them show up to ride at our little bush track.

We were even more shocked to hear the conditions of that race.

Out of their own pockets, the horse owners and backers of each respective horse put up more money than I had ever seen before. Ronnie and Randy competed in a $10,000 race that was only 36 feet long! Over 200 people stood at the starting gate, probably feeling as excited and astounded as I was.

The gates opened, the horses took off, and just like that it was over. Randy's horse won $10,000 for less than five seconds of work. Ronnie wasn't nearly as experienced as Randy was and it sure cost him – even though it was only a five second race.

As unconventional as that race was, I think Calvin and I both agreed that we would love to participate in something that grand one day.

At that time, the races that Calvin and I rode in were tiny and barely paid any money. Most of the time we each made about $5 or $10 on a race, and we were very happy to make that. Every once in a while we could get a tip if we did a great job and the owners made a big profit off of us. But for the most part, we were making next to nothing. Still, we were happy to make any money we could and we were even happier that we had such a fun time while we made our money. We enjoyed ourselves so much that sometimes we even rode for free; it really was that much fun.

The problem was that just like everything else in my life, my dad took control of my finances.

There I was, a 12-year-old kid, and I was helping to feed my family. When I'd come home from Clement's, I had to give my dad all of the money I had earned. And he knew I had it because he would come to the races, still drunk from the night before, with a beer in his hand to watch me.

As soon as we got home, I had to give him my little envelope of cash and he might give me a dollar or two out of it. He told me that he was saving money for me to get a car and that's why he took so much of my money.

At this point, I was making my own money and I wanted to keep it. I wanted to be able to go out and do things because I worked for the privilege to do so. You would have never known how hard I worked, though. My dad took almost every cent I made and he did whatever he wanted to do with it.

When I went to school, I ate free lunch, so that was not a financial obstacle. But sometimes I wanted a snack. I just wanted to buy some chips or cookies or candy. I was a kid and I wanted to eat the things that the other kids ate — especially since I made the money to afford it.

Unfortunately, my dad just didn't care.

Since my father was always out drinking and he would eventually knock himself out cold, I had to go to pretty extreme measures to take back a portion of what was rightfully mine. I watched him while he slept, making sure that he wouldn't move. If I got caught doing what I planned to do, no amount of boxing matches could have saved me.

So I acted as quickly and quietly as we did when we went outlawing for rabbits. I crept up on my father while he was sleeping and I don't think I breathed the entire time. When I was sure that he was completely out of it, I would reach into his knit pants and grab whatever change I could find. If I felt a quarter, I would take it and run.

That's right. I robbed his ass.

He took mine and I was determined to take his – if you can even call it that. My dad barely ever made any money. He acted like he was all big and bad, but in my eyes, he was nothing. What kind of man doesn't take care of his family?

I brought in a little bit of cash with my races, but my mom was the real bread winner of the Sellers house. My father lived off our money and kept us from spending any of it. I watched my mom walk to work because my dad was still out drinking from the night before.

He was literally drinking our money away.

I'm not proud to say that I stole from him, but if taking your own money is considered stealing, then I was happy to steal. What I did was not nearly as wrong as what my dad did to us. I'm not proud that I had to pick through his pockets for spare change, but he shouldn't be proud for most of the things he did as a father, either.

You don't rob your kids. You just don't do that. You don't do that to any kid, no matter how bad he or she may be. But my dad robbed me, his own son; his son that did anything his father asked of him. If one thing was for sure, it was that I would never treat my family the way he did.

I couldn't stand to watch him drinking the money he took from me and the money my mother worked so hard for away. I hated the way he treated my mama and I hated the way he treated us kids. I hated everything about him.

And as much as I hated everything that he did, there was one thing I hated even more. I hated the fact that I loved him so much.

Whether or not he knew it, my dad was killing all of us from the inside out. He treated us like we were dirt; like we were nothing. He did it to my older brother, he did it to my mother, and he did it to me.

Since he didn't see anything wrong with his actions, it didn't look like they would stop any time soon.

If I wanted to keep my sanity, I needed to get out of there. I saw what my dad did to Keith and I didn't want that to happen to me. There would have to be a point when I could just pack up my shit and flip my dad the proverbial bird.

As it turned out, that point didn't come until four years later. I was still racing, but I was still going through the same problems at home that I went through as a child. I knew then more than ever that I needed to leave and I needed to leave fast.

The only problem was I had nowhere to go. Even if I did have a place to go, I didn't have the money to get there. I was still earning money at the bush tracks, but it was time for me to get my jockeys license and figure out where I was going to ride and how to afford it. If I wanted to get out of that hellhole, I needed to step my game up and expand my horizons.

So that's exactly what I did.

When I was 16 years old, I was still riding at the bush track, but I also found other forms of income. I met some people who paid me to work their horses after school, so that was really helpful. Not only could I stay away from my house when I got out of school, but I got to make some extra money doing it. The best part was that I was still working with horses and that's all I ever wanted to do.

By then I was well on my way to becoming a professional athlete. Once I got my racing license, I started riding at Evangeline Downs, a small, but officially-sanctioned track about 25 miles of Erath, in Lafayette, Louisiana. Riding at Evangeline was wonderful for me because I built up a lot of experience and I started making much more money.

But all that meant was that my dad was stealing much more money from me.

Every time I got my check, I cashed it in at the race track and put the money in an envelope. I couldn't touch a single penny of what was in that envelope until I got home and gave it to my father.

He would look in the envelope and suddenly he thought he was an accountant; a visual mathematician.

My dad would put money in different envelopes for my to pay my kitchen bill, my valet, and my agent. Then he would tell me that I owed him this much for my food, that much for my electric bill, and this much for my rent. Hell, I'm surprised that he didn't charge me a fee for breathing on his property.

Once my dad deducted all of my "expenses," he would give me about $100 and keep the rest for himself. He told me he was saving that money so he could buy me a car and so I would have money when I was ready to move out of my house. I hoped he was telling the truth, but I highly doubted he was.

There I was working a ton of jobs and that son of a bitch was taking all of my money to go out drinking. There was nothing I could do, though, so I continued running around like a madman and working my ass off every day. I worked some horses before school, went to my classes, worked at other farms after school, did my homework, worked at the bush track, and raced whenever I could.

Then I handed all of my money to my dad and woke up the next day to start the whole cycle all over again.

I think the only thing that got me through that period is that I could race a lot more than I did before since I finally had my racing license. I still raced at Clement's and I spent a lot of time at Evangeline Downs. When I wasn't racing, I still cared for horses and exercised them as much as I could.

Just like when I was a kid, I wanted to be with horses as often as time would allow and I was finally in a position to do that. I was really thankful for every turn my life took. If it wasn't for the horrible circumstances at home, I would have been truly happy.

Then one day out of the clear blue sky, it was like the Heavens opened up and God heard my cries.

A guy named Terry Romero asked me if I wanted to live together in a camper trailer. He said he would talk to my father and that I would finally be able to get out of my house. Needless to say, it didn't take me long to take him up on his offer.

So I sat my dad down and told him that I wanted to leave home; that I wanted to get out of there. I asked him if I could have the money he had been saving for me and he laughed. Then he said, "I ain't got no money for ya, but as long as you keep your grades up and keep pulling in A's and B's, you're free to go."

Those were the sweetest words I ever heard.

I was free to leave. Free to leave the chaos, the madness. Free to leave the mental abuse and the physical labor. Free to leave the sounds of everyone crying while my dad went on another drunken rampage.

Free.

So I packed up my things, I made one more mental curse that my father had all my money, I said goodbye to my family, and I got the hell out of there as fast as I could. I didn't have any money and I didn't care.

After all, the best things in life are free.

And so was I.

Part 2

A Prince Within the Sport of Kings

Chapter 7

When I started riding more frequently at Evangeline Downs, I knew I was well on my way to becoming a professional athlete. What I didn't realize was that I was also well on my way to becoming a professional heaver.

By the time I turned 17, my body was growing and it was growing fast. All of a sudden, it was becoming a problem for me to be *light* enough to meet the required weight my horse must carry. As an 11-year-old I had had to stuff lead in my saddle to ride. Now it was like I was carrying the lead in my body.

Now don't get me wrong. I wasn't overweight or heavy by any means. However, I needed to weigh about 112 pounds to be able to ride.

Weight assignments vary from race to race, but a typical "impost" – what the horse must carry on its back – is about 115 pounds. That includes the 112 pound rider, plus everything else. The list begins with the rider's "silks," which is a sheer uniform shirt in the registered colors of the horse's owner, plus pants, boots, and saddle. The saddles we use might look substantial to a fan in the grandstand, but they're just patent leather, and weigh as little as two pounds, including aluminum stirrups – a total of about three pounds.

So I needed to weigh no more than 112 pounds, naked, and maintaining such a low weight while my body was still growing seemed almost impossible. I felt like I was getting heavier by the day and I didn't know how to cope with that fact. My predicament was especially hard because I *had* to make weight because I *had* to be a jockey. There was no alternative. After all, this was all I knew since I was 11 years old and I gave up my education to become a professional jockey. I was stuck; I was in it.

After I moved out of my house, I became so involved in horse racing that I didn't have time for much else. When I was a senior in high school, I would go to work in the morning, work my horses, go back to my trailer to take a shower, go to school, come home, do my homework, and go to sleep. Then there was night racing. I would sleep for two hours and go to the jocks' room to ride at night.

Almost every day was a battle because I was doing too much, and the kids at school were jealous because I had a real job and my own car. That continued until about two weeks before the end of my senior year. I was really struggling and my dad let me quit. I gave up all my A's and B's because riding was more important to me. I wanted to be a jockey at any cost. But as the pounds piled on, and it became harder to take them off, I quickly learned that I may have severed my life's options at too young of an age.

As it turned out, I was not alone. Most of the jocks at Evangeline Downs had the same kind of problems I did, but they also had something that I didn't have; they had a solution. It may not have been the best solution, but it sure did work.

Pretty soon after I started riding full-time, some of the jockeys took me under their wing and showed me the easiest way to make weight. In other words, they taught me how to make myself throw up everything I had just eaten. When they first pitched the idea to me, it didn't even seem odd. I was willing to do whatever I could to make weight, so I made it a point to do just that.

The riders who had been heaving for a while, were full of valuable advice on the best ways to heave. They would say, "If you're gonna heave, make sure you eat a lot. Eat as much as you can and get as full as you can."

Others would say, "Get yourself real full and drink plenty of liquids because that will help everything come right up."

Then some of the older riders who had been heaving for decades would give little tips and tricks. One jock told me, "Try drinking some coffee or a warm cup of water before you heave. Everything will come up much easier that way."

Everyone had their secrets of heaving and we passed them around the jocks' room like a bunch of boys telling ghost stories around a campfire. And even though our stories didn't actually have any ghosts, they sure were scary.

I'll never forget my first time kneeling in front of a toilet bowl with my finger down my throat, trying to get rid of the food I just paid for in the jocks' room kitchen. I wiggled my finger this way and that, stroking the back of my tongue, swirling around my uvula, and rubbing every part of my throat that I could reach. It took a while, but eventually I felt my throat contract and the inevitable feeling you get in the pit of your stomach when you're about to be sick. As soon as that feeling came, I was spewing out a combination of half digested cheeseburger and burning green bile. The feeling was simultaneously terrible and relieving.

As much as I disliked the heaving process, I was happy that I could eat and still make weight. How ironic. Food was scarce when I was a kid and now I was finally in a position to eat whatever I wanted – but only if I wanted to lose my job. Even though I couldn't fully enjoy my food because I had to flip, I was at least happy to know that I could bask in the taste of all the foods that smelled up the jocks' room kitchen before I had to throw it up again.

Of course, flipping, as jockeys like to call it, was not enough to keep my weight down. My fellow jockeys also taught me the secrets of the sweat box. This was not the kind of sauna that you would find at a gym, or a health spa. In those days, the sweat box, or hot box as we called it, was restricting to the point where a person could develop claustrophobia.

I remember stepping into the box and taking a deep breath while the hot air consumed me. Armed with a pail that contained some ice, some water, and a sponge, I got ready to sweat off as much weight as I could. I would stay there for hours with sweat pouring off my body and pooling in a warm puddle around my feet. If I started to feel dizzy, I would squeeze the ice-cold water over my head with the sponge. Then I would bite on the sponge, feel the cool water hit my tongue, and have to spit it back out. Feeling as thirsty as I was, that was torture.

When it finally got to be enough – too much – I got out and wiped myself down with a towel. Then I stepped into a dwarf-sized whirlpool for a minute to make my body extra hot before I got back in the box again.

Imagine that. My freedom from my home life became my body's own prison.

At the time, I didn't really see it that way. I was just happy to spend my time with the horses and to be able to ride. Plus, I really enjoyed making friends with the jockeys who taught me the ropes of horse racing.

During the beginning of my career, I was thrilled that I still got to spend time with my childhood buddies Kenny Desarmeaux and Calvin Borel, and make new friends with jockeys like Ken Patin. Not only were Calvin and Ken fun to hang out with, but it was also a joy to ride against them. Evangeline Downs had a lot of great riders from Louisiana and I became terrific friends with all of them.

As time went on, I turned flipping into an art form. I didn't have to swirl my finger down my throat, choking and gagging as I did in the old days. In fact, I didn't need to use my finger at all. I just had to bend over a bit, open my mouth, and let the rush of food and bile flow out. Then, unlike my earlier days when I had to squat down to recuperate, I just got up and walked away as if nothing ever happened.

The same rules applied to my time in the hot box. Fortunately, when I started riding, there weren't many of the old-fashioned hot boxes left. Most jockeys didn't have to sit alone in a box with their heads hanging out as if they were waiting for a swift execution in the guillotine. Instead, we all got to kill ourselves slowly by draining all the water out of our systems in a sauna the size of the room. This change could have been because technology was better. Or it could have been because it was more cost effective to fit a bunch of jockeys in one big hot box. However, if you ask me, the change came about because of what happened to Randy Romero.

In 1983, Louisiana jockey hero Randy Romero, who was fast becoming a big star on the national scene, rubbed himself down with alcohol and got in the old style hot box. He was doing just what he or any other jockey would do on a normal day. But as that particular day showed, there was nothing normal about being in one of those hot boxes. Randy accidentally bumped into one of the burning bulbs, shattering it into a cascade of sharp glass shards. As his body came into contact with wires in the live bulb, a fierce fire erupted, with the alcohol suddenly igniting. Randy became a flailing fire ball as flames raged over his body. I think the only thing that was not horribly burned was his face because of the style of those sweat boxes.

Amazingly enough, Randy survived his accident and was able to resume riding after he had a few blood transfusions and his skin healed. It was a long and painful recovery which left him scarred by the burns over much of his body. As horrified as the rest of us were by what happened to Randy, the show had to go on. Word of Randy's accident must have reached every jockey's ear at every race track. It was all we could talk about.

"Can you believe what happened to Randy?"

"Maybe we should stick with baby oil."

"Those fucking hot boxes …"

And one question that crossed all of our minds that none of us really wanted to voice was "Is this going to happen to *me*?"

But even with our fears at an all time high, we had to push them to the side. We were jockeys, and the hot box was just a part of the job. Like it or not, it was something we all had to utilize.

I'll never forget the smell of musty baby oil lingering in the hot box while we jockeys all sat together and talked. Living life like Adam before he realized he was naked, we all sat there in our birthday suits, lathering ourselves in baby oil or rubbing on alcohol to make our bodies sweat harder. That baby oil closed up our pores like nothing else and let the sweat pour off us in a steady stream. I used to rub my hands down my arms, legs, and torso, literally pulling the sweat off my body. Perhaps that's where the track term "pulling weight" came from. In any case, we would sweat so much that we had to physically help the streaming waterfalls plop onto the wooden floor.

It might not sound like spending time in a sauna would be all that bad, but believe me, it was. Even though most hot boxes had the standard warning that told us to get out after 30 minutes or one hour, nobody followed those rules. No one at the tracks enforced those rules, either. After all, jockeys needed to be light, and the higher officials were not about to put *our* health before *their* races.

So we sat in the hot box as often as we could for as long as our bodies would allow. You'd see a jockey leave the box, but return a few minutes later, muttering something like, "Damn, still another two pounds to go."

Another jockey would respond, "Yeah? Don't complain. I have to pull another three."

"Hey," another would say, "I'm still weighing in at '22. Stop your bitching."

Then the jocks who were too tired to even comment would nod their heads in agreement and continue to sit and sweat until they finally knew they could get on the scale with confidence.

There are, of course, jockeys who are small enough that they don't have to sweat off pounds to make weight. The late Bill Shoemaker, who retired as the winningest rider in history, was a naturally small man who didn't tip the scales at an ounce over a hundred pounds. But most men that size don't possess the raw strength needed to handle a thoroughbred racehorse that might weigh 1,000 pounds. The Shoe was an exception. Pat Day was another top rider like that. He'd been a competitive wrestler in high school, and was a great athlete. Both of these jockeys had what it took to ride and they had the bodies to match their talents, but they were the exceptions to the rule.

Women weigh less than men, and a good amount of them have broken into the sport in recent years. But most of the jocks are men, who if they watched their calories, might naturally weigh around 130-135 pounds like a lightweight in boxing. And so jockeys rely on drastic diets and dangerous reducing techniques like heaving and sweating to take 20 pounds off to ride professionally. And 20 pounds for a guy who would be slim at 130, is like a 200-pounder trying to make 150.

It wasn't natural, but that's what most of us had to do to ride.

Sometimes I would stay in the sweat box for so long that I shed three, four, or five pounds in one session. Other jocks might pull seven or eight pounds. On the days when I pulled a lot of weight, I could barely even function when I got out of the box. I would lean my head against a bench while my body silently begged for water. My lips and mouth were so dry that I would have drunk my own sweat if I thought it would help. Running my parched tongue over my dry lips, all I could think about was the cool refreshment that I could get from a bottle of water, or even a *sip* of water. Hell, even dabbing my lips with a wet paper towel would have helped. But I couldn't have any of those things. Any liquid I would drink would have defeated the purpose of getting in the hot box to begin with.

When the time came, I had to pick my head up off the bench and try to ignore my dehydration and starvation long enough to stand on level ground without my legs giving out beneath me. I would get on the scale, see the progress I had made, and prepare to mount a horse. All the while I felt like I was in a drunken stupor without having the brief pleasure of drinking the liquor – or anything else for that matter.

That's the way things were every day. The other jockeys and I heaved, we sweated, and we barely ate. We took diet pills and laxatives just as often as we took over-the-counter or prescription water pills. Basically, we did everything we could to shed off any excess pounds before a race. In a way, it was like we worked for the dieting industry instead of the horse racing industry.

But that was all just a part of being a jockey. If you wanted to ride, you had to make weight. And if you wanted to make weight, chances were that you would have to pull weight. That's the way things were then and that's the way things still are now. Or at least that's the way things are for the jockeys who agree to play by horse racing's outdated rules.

Chapter 8

Back when I rode at the bush track, I thought my career would soar once I could ride at sanctioned racetracks. I thought every track was like Churchill Downs; that every race would be like the Kentucky Derby. As time proved, I couldn't have been more wrong.

During my first few years of riding, I went back and forth between Evangeline Downs and Delta Downs, another small track in Louisiana. The people there were very nice, but I couldn't say the same for the tracks themselves. More importantly, I couldn't say the same about the horses.

The horses at Evangeline and Delta were not like the ones I saw in those old Westerns, nor were they like what I saw on TV racing. The horses at those small tracks in Louisiana were just plain bad. Either they couldn't run or they were crippled. I know that wasn't their fault, but it did make things extra hard for me as a rider.

When you ride good horses, they jump right up underneath and it's just a matter of you pointing them in the right direction. But when you ride bad horses, they won't get underneath you. They're either too sore or they just can't run.

But I never wanted to force a horse. Even though I rode with a stick – a whip – I used it as little as possible. For me, it wasn't just go-go-go every step of the way. If you blast a horse out of the gate at top speed and let him run as fast as he can, he's not likely to last. I considered myself a *tactical* speed rider. That's what I was taught to do and I liked that style of riding. I could control speed horses and adjust the pace of the race to best suit my horse; try to save something for when I would need it in the race.

That was not the case at Evangeline Downs. I would holler at the horses to make them run, like I did in my very first race. You could beat on them with your whip and holler all you wanted, but they just didn't want to run.

So what did I do? I adjusted my riding style and went against my morals to do what every other rider did there.

Simply put, I shocked those horses into running – literally.

In the world of horse racing, there are certain tools and tactics that a jockey should never use. The top tool on that list is the buzzer, or the machine. This machine is about the size of standard lighter and it uses two little AA batteries that are stuck together with black tape. The machine has two prongs at the end. When the prong presses into the horse's hide it causes a shock, like one of those gag hand-shaking buzzers. Only stronger. If you press that machine into a horse's neck right there where you are holding the reins, it shocks the hell out of the horse and makes it run like crazy.

I was never one to resort to electronics – especially not illegal ones – to make a horse run. But at Evangeline, that was what I was expected to do; that was what I *had* to do. All of the riders there used a machine in those days, so if I tried to stray from the norm, I wouldn't get any mounts. Since I needed to make a living out of racing and most races only put about $50 in my pocket, I needed as many mounts as I could get.

So against my better judgment, I used the machine. All of us jockeys used our machines on the sour horses who didn't want to run anymore and on the crippled horses that hurt too badly to run. With just a little jolt, the horses would run out of their skin for us. The actual shock didn't hurt the horses, but making crippled ones run faster wasn't right. I knew it was cruel. I knew it was wrong. But I also knew that I didn't have another choice if I wanted to ride. Just like heaving, there are some things that you just have to accept if you want to be a rider.

But even with all of my heaving, sweating, and shocking, I was still getting nowhere quickly. I was stuck traveling back and forth to Evangeline or Delta Downs, depending on the season. Basically, I was stuck between a rock and a hard place. I wasn't winning many races and it looked like I was never going to.

Despite my knack for losing, I still had a lot of support behind me. Back at Evangeline, a teenage girl named Kelli was always at the track to cheer me on, though I suspected that she was much more interested in the races because her father owned horses and she was infatuated with Calvin. A lot of other people supported me and cheered me on, too. People kept telling me that I needed to get out of there; that I had a shot and I could make it big. So I could stay there and be a jockey or I could do as everybody had been telling me to do and get out of there to go make something of myself.

After a while, I went up to Oaklawn Park, which is a big track in Hot Springs, Arkansas, but that didn't change my luck any. I was still a small fish in an even bigger pond, and I didn't get many horses to ride because I didn't have an agent. So I wasn't quite sure of what to expect in my future.

One day I was talking to was Melvin Holland, a fellow jockey in Hot Springs, and I said, "Melvin, I'm disgusted by all this. What am I supposed to do?"

Melvin looked me square in the eye and said, "Shane, Don't get disgusted. You can ride. The perfect place for you is Fairmount Park in Illinois. Go over there. You'll win races and your talent will do the rest."

I thought about what he said and I decided that maybe Melvin was right. Maybe I could win some races and be the kind of jockey I wanted to be. So I made up my mind and decided to leave Louisiana and Arkansas. I was going north to Illinois and nothing could stop me.

On the last day of the race meeting at Hot Springs, I worked some horses for trainer Don Newcomb and he asked if I wanted to ride one. He had a horse that was sore and was dropping down in class. Don couldn't find anyone to ride him, so he offered me the opportunity at the last minute. Since it was my last day, I was more than happy to take Don up on his offer.

When the gates opened, the horse didn't have any speed. He dropped back to fifth and I could only watch through the rain as the other horses sped ahead of us. Mud splattered all over my goggles and I thanked God that I had plenty of spare goggles under the top set. A jockey stacks several pairs of goggles together and starts the race looking through all of them. When a set is covered with mud being thrown back by the hooves of the horses in front of him, the rider simply peels off the top set and begins with a fresh view.

It was a really sloppy-muddy track that day, and as more and more mud came back at me, I pulled my goggles down around my neck over and over again. I was down to my last two pairs in the middle of the turn, at which point I was laying third. I knew I only had two pairs of goggles left so I swung my horse to the outside of the two horses in front of me. Then I pulled down another set of goggles and I only had one pair left. But by then my view was clear. My horse ran to the front of the pack and I came in first with my last pair of goggles. I won that race by myself – no machine, no spare goggles, but a whole lot of self-confidence.

When I jumped off my new favorite horse, everyone wanted to give me their congratulations. Melvin tipped his hat to me and winked. The other jockeys patted me on the back and said things like "Good race," or "You've been holding back on us 'til your last day, you bastard!" All of their comments were in good nature and I knew that they were happy for me. That was the perfect way for me to end the meet at Hot Springs, and I wouldn't change it for anything in the world.

I was headed for a smaller track at Fairmount Park, which is across the Mississippi River from St. Louis, in Illinois, but that could mean more chances to ride, and the chance to make a name for myself.

Before I left Hot Springs, some of the jockeys and trainers gave me a bit of advice. They told me about a man I had never heard of before named Dave Gall, and said that he was the only thing I had to worry about once I got to Fairmount. He had been leading rider there for over 20 years and won over 6,000 races. Even though he was in his 50s, he could still ride like a 20-year-old.

I wouldn't admit it to my fellow jockeys at the time, but I was terrified to meet that man. When I got to Fairmount, I expected to meet a monster, but what I found was a thin little man. Despite all the stories I heard, Dave Gall was a very quiet person for whom I held nothing but respect. I couldn't have been happier to find out that the man I expected to be my arch nemesis would turn out to be my friend.

I started riding against him and I still think he was one of my greatest competitors throughout my career. Dave and I started challenging each other right away, race riding the best we could. He appreciated that. Other than Nelson Medina and me, Dave didn't have anyone else to give him a real run for his money. The three of us rode the best horses and I think we all brought out the best in each other.

Outside of Dave, Nelson was the jockey I looked up to the most. He looked amazing on a horse; he was like the picture image of what a jockey should look like. I thought he was one of the best riders I had ever met, both on and off the track. Not only was he an incredible rider, but he was also a great friend.

During our first meet, Dave kept his title as leading rider and I came in second. But the second time around, I beat him and I became the leading rider. I was finally going somewhere and Dave respected me for that.

In retrospect, I just wish I had paid more attention to where I was going.

Right as I was wrapping up the riding title, I was walking around Fairmount Park with an agent, just talking and not paying attention to much else. I remember it was freezing outside that day and I was looking at the agent while I tried to keep my hands warm in my pockets. Aside from the cold and my conversation, I was oblivious to what was going on around me.

However, I took in my surroundings really quickly when I turned around and a horse kicked me right in the face. With the wind knocked out of me, I fell backwards and landed on the cold ground. All of my senses were taken over by agony. I felt like my face was falling off and it was only held together by the shreds of sharp pain. All I could see was a combination of red and white as blood streamed down my face and puffs of cold-induced steam cascaded from the bloody mess.

I was still pretty much oblivious at the hospital. When the doctors saw me and I saw their noses wrinkle in concern, I knew that my condition was just as serious as I imagined it to be. The three pieces of skin that previously secured my nose to my face were ripped, leaving my nose flapping in the air. The skin above my upper lip was torn, making it look almost like I had a second mouth. My face was ruined and I couldn't even care because the pain was so severe. It was unbearable.

After my injury, I went through some reconstructive surgery and the doctors put me back together like I was a lucky Humpty Dumpty. I went back home to Louisiana while I recovered and entire civilizations could have risen and fallen while I waited to get better.

Then one day when I finally felt a bit more human, I decided to go out and see some of the people I had missed while I was away in Illinois. To my surprise, one of the first people I saw was a lovely young lady named Melanie. She was my first girlfriend when I was 11 years old, and nine years later, I felt like we had never left each other's side. We started dating again and before I knew it, I was married at the age of 20.

When I fully recovered, Melanie came back to Fairmount with me and we quickly went from being childhood sweethearts to being an old married couple. After six months, it became obvious that we got married too young and too fast. Melanie stayed with me for almost a whole race meeting and then we parted ways with a divorce. It was a sad divorce – a painful one – but we didn't fight about it. Both of us knew that we were just too young and that our unexpected marriage wasn't meant to be.

So before I was even old enough to bet on the races I was riding, I learned two very important lessons. One: Never get kicked in the face by a horse. Two: Never get married if you do.

And in all my years, those are two of the most important lessons I've ever learned.

Chapter 9

Soon after Melanie and I finalized our divorce, I started a new chapter in my life – no pun intended.

While I was at Fairmount, I ran across an old friend named C.D. Delahoussaye, a trainer I'd known back in Louisiana. So I was really happy to see him. I was even happier to see a guy named Breezy who I knew from when I was a kid. Aside from me, they were the only guys from Louisiana I knew in Illinois, so their presence made me feel right at home – without my dad ruining things, of course.

From that moment on, I spent most of my free time and a lot of my working time with C.D. and Breezy. We became even better friends than we were in Louisiana and we spent hour after hour laughing and having fun. Breezy was a real character and he made it hard for us not to be in a great mood all the time. He was as dark as the ace of spades and his teeth were as white as snow. We used to joke around with him when it was dark out and say that if it wasn't for those shiny white teeth, we wouldn't be able to find him in the dark. Breezy would laugh and crack jokes back at us and we all felt like we were kids again.

Breezy became my exercise boy and I would pay him with what he liked best – cash and liquor. He was an alcoholic, but a real happy one. In the mornings, I would get a horse at Fairmount and then I would leave with Breezy to go work horses at an old track named Cahokia Downs. On the way to Cahokia, we always had to stop at a liquor store so I could get him a bottle of Strawberry Hill wine. He would take a sip from the bottle, roll his eyes way up into his head so the whites shone like reflectors, and make his trademark "Goot-gooda-lee-goo" sound. Then he'd straighten his body right up and say, "I'm ready now Boss Man. We gotta get going." With that, he would tuck the bottle away for later and get right to work.

The first horse Breezy ponied me on at Fairmount Park was named Fred and I. Back at Evangeline Downs, the horse hadn't won a lot of races. I really respected his owner C.B., also known as Papa C, and never used a machine on him back at home.

When Breezy and I worked with the horse, he hadn't won in three or four starts. We knew he was a front runner and that he had potential; he just wouldn't win. When we got him in the post parade, I was really nervous because he was one of my first decent shot horses. I wanted him to win, but Breezy and I both knew that the chances of that happening were slim.

Breezy was ponying the horse for me and we were trying to prepare for the big race. Out of nowhere, Breezy turned to me and said, "Look Boss," and pulled out a machine. Apparently he had been hiding the machine next to what must have been an empty liquor bottle, because he was drunk and clearly out of his mind.

I pushed Breezy's hand down and loudly whispered, "Put that thing away, man! I ain't riding the horse with that thing!" That machine terrified me and I didn't want anybody else to see it.

Breezy's voice became a bit desperate as he said, "Come on, Boss. I need you to win this race. I bet 20 bucks on it!"

Keeping my voice as low as my anger was high, I replied, "Breezy, put that fucking thing away! Where'd you get that thing from?" At that point I was terrified. This wasn't like Louisiana where you would get a slap on the wrist for using a machine. You could get a lifetime suspension over here. I continued, "Put that thing away before I tell Papa C. We don't even know where we're at over here and you want to go waving that thing all around!"

Breezy saw that I was serious and he finally put the machine away. Still irritated and more than a little scared, I kept my mouth shut as we went into the starting gate. Then, as fast as Breezy had pulled out his machine, the horses were off and I was flying. Against all odds, Fred and I was winning and he was winning by a landslide.

Meanwhile, Breezy was standing with the other pony boys on the turn, cheering me and the horse on. While he was standing there, he somehow dropped the machine on the ground, right in front of a veterinarian. Breezy picked up the machine and stuck it in his boot, but he was too late. The vet saw the machine and called the stewards to tell them what he witnessed.

While all that was happening, I won the race the right way; the fair way. I got off the horse, had my picture taken, and then prepared to celebrate. Before I got the chance to even smile, someone came over and said, "Shane, the stewards want to talk to you."

More than a little nervous, I got on the phone and the stewards said, "You're off all your mounts."

Shocked, I repeated, "I'm off all my mounts?" I wondered what the hell had happened in the two minutes that I was racing.

Suddenly I was surrounded by security guards and I knew I was in some serious trouble. Security had searched Breezy and they found him with the machine in his boot. When they questioned him, he was scared and said that it was mine. The security guards told me what Breezy said and at that moment, I could have killed him for lying. I tried to explain that I was scared when I saw the machine and that I didn't use it, but they didn't care. Without a second thought, they suspended me and I knew there was a good chance that I could be ruled off for life.

At that point, I didn't know what I would do; what I *could* do. I only had $3,500 and I knew that wasn't going to get me very far. I certainly couldn't call my parents for money and I had too much pride to ask anyone else for help. At that point, there was nobody for me to turn to.

Thankfully, I didn't have to turn too far because two weeks after I was ruled off, my friend Steve Elzy stepped in. He was an agent and he actually wanted to take my book and represent me. Better yet, he wanted to let me stay with him until I could get back on my feet again.

I had never been so thankful. Before Steve, I hadn't ridden for two weeks and I was starving. I was living off of beanie weenies and macaroni, not caring about things like calories since I couldn't ride, anyway. So when Steve offered to help me, I couldn't take him up on his offer fast enough.

One day, Steve turned to me and said, "You're a riding son of a bitch. We need to get you back on a horse."

Though I appreciated the sentiment, the only thing I could reply with was, "I can't ride anywhere but in Illinois."

Thinking nothing of it, Steve said, "That's bullshit. Let's go to Kentucky." He continued, "But first, we need to get you a lawyer and file for an injunction."

I said, "Okay, then. Let's do it."

Without a second thought, we got in the car and went to Ellis Park, one of the greatest tracks I had ever seen up until that point. I was named to ride on six horses my first day there, so it looked like things were going to get better. But I couldn't escape the law – Murphy's Law included – and I couldn't get a license to ride in Kentucky. Because of my injunction, I couldn't ride outside the state of Illinois and the stewards denied me my license.

More discouraged than ever, Steve and I went all the way back to Illinois and I returned to Fairmount. I appealed the ruling in Illinois and tried to get an injunction. Finally, I was reinstated and all charges were dropped. But as happy as I was, I still couldn't let go of the fact that I had been booted from the game to begin with.

When I got reinstated, the first thing I wanted to do was find Breezy. I was mad at him, but I still loved him, so I didn't know what I would do when I finally found him. I asked about him everywhere I went, trying my best to find where he was. And when

I finally found him, I couldn't help but let my love overpower my anger.

I opened the door to a barn at Cahokia Downs and saw Breezy sleeping on top of a bail of hay with a towel covering him. When he heard the door open and the light came in, he jumped up like he was terrified. As soon as he saw me standing there, Breezy started to cry. He cried and cried, making me think back on all of the old times when we did nothing but laugh together. Before I opened that door, I wanted to hit him, but now, I just wanted to hug him.

Breezy's voice shook with sadness and remorse as he said, "I'm so sorry Boss Man. They said they was gonna put me in jail and that I would never be able to go home." Between sobs, he continued, "I was scared that they weren't going to let me go home so I told them what they wanted to hear. I just wanted to go home." Then he just kept crying and I started crying with him.

That was one of the most painful things I ever witnessed. I knew Breezy was scared and that he just wanted to go back home. He was sick with alcoholism, he didn't know how to read or write, and he didn't know anybody in Illinois. All he wanted to do was go back home.

After seeing him like that, I knew I had to let bygones be bygones. I got Breezy a ride in a horse van headed back home to Louisiana and I gave him a big hug before he left. At the time, I thought I was saving him; saving him from his loneliness, from his guilt, and most of all, from himself. When I watched the van drive away, I made a mental prayer for Breezy to get better. I couldn't have known it then, but Breezy would never get better. Two years after I said goodbye to one of my dearest friends, he died from cirrhosis of the liver. And if I knew Breezy, I was willing to bet that he passed on with his big, white smile that could light up a room.

Of course, I didn't know what was in store for Breezy on the night he left Illinois. All I knew was that I was allowed to ride again and that I was going to do everything in my power to make sure that everything about my career was honest. The meet was over, I was leading rider, and I was going to go to Chicago. But first, I decided to spend a bit of time at home and go back to Louisiana.

It had been a few years since I last rode at the Fairgrounds, a major track in New Orleans, but not much had changed. The only big change I saw was in the teenage girl who used to cheer me on and still went to the races every day. Kelli was no longer a teenager with a case of puppy love for Calvin. Now she was a full-blown woman and she was the prettiest woman I had ever seen. She had long black hair, shinier than a new car, and she wore it all puffed up like women did back in those days. Everything about her was gorgeous and I was instantly hooked.

Knowing that I was divorced, Kelli gave me her phone number and we agreed to talk soon. As it turned out, we ended up talking a lot. The people at the track had to have seen what was blossoming between us because they were the ones who basically set us up. One day I won a race for Louis Rousell, the owner of the

Fairgrounds, and he called me over to the barn after the race. He nudged his head in Kelli's direction, gave me $100, and said for me to go out and have some fun. So that's exactly what we did. Kelli and I went to some bars in New Orleans and we had a great time. From that moment on, I knew that my first marriage was doomed to fail because I was destined to be with this woman for the rest of my life.

Happier than I could ever remember being, I spent all of my time riding or being with Kelli. Now I truly knew what love was, but now I also had to make a decision between real love and my love for horse racing.

I was excited that it was time to return to Illinois to ride, but I was also very upset that I would have to leave Kelli. We promised that we would talk all the time and visit each other as often as possible. And even though those were only words, I knew that they would become real actions.

So I kept riding and talking on the phone with Kelli, just as we had promised to do. Even with the distance between us, I felt closer to her than I ever had before. She lit my torch of motivation and I still think it was her love that helped me win so many races.

And since I became leading rider that year, I knew that meant that Kelli loved me a whole lot.

Chapter 10

Once I became leading rider at Fairmount, I was ready to move on to bigger and better things. I wound up in Chicago, one of the greatest racing cities in the country, and I couldn't have been happier. There I was, a small town boy living in the big city – and the only thing I was missing was my small town girl from back home.

While I lived in Chicago, Kelli visited me as often as she could. But even with all the visits and all the phone calls, it wasn't enough. I wanted to be with Kelli and she wanted to be with me just as much. So after a while of missing each other as much as we loved each other, Kelli packed up her bags and moved in with me.

At that point, my life couldn't have been more perfect. I was riding at Sportsman's Park, which is one of three big thoroughbred race tracks in Chicago, along with Hawthorne Race Course and Arlington Park. The three tracks rotated their race meetings so there was no overlap, and there was always a racetrack open. It was the "Chicago circuit," like I'd been on the small-track Louisiana circuit at Evangeline and Delta Downs, only this was big-city Chicago.

Every day seemed to bring more friends. Right after I started riding there, I was thrilled to see that I would be riding with Nelson Medina again. We were both new to Illinois, so it was really nice to have someone to travel around with from Fairmount to Sportsman's Park to Arlington Park. Even when he had a rough day or we spent too much time together in the hot box, Nelson was always there with a smile. He was like my sounding board and he made me feel like even the biggest catastrophe wasn't really all that bad.

Around the same time, I also became great friends with jockey Mike Smith. I had originally met Mike in Hot Springs, but our relationship then consisted only of nods of acknowledgment. Once we started riding together in Chicago, I saw that he was a real cool cat and he quickly became the best friend I had – except for Kelli, of course.

I became fantastic friends with Kerwin Clark, another terrific jockey, too. We had great times together and things only got better once Mark Guidry and Robby Albarado came to Chicago. Before long, Mike, Mark, Robby, and Kerwin became more than friends to me; they became like brothers. We spent so much time together on the track and in the hot box that we were practically inseparable. I barely ever spoke to my family back in Louisiana, so I felt blessed every day because I had formed such an incredible family of my own.

That was also around the time when I met Frankie Brothers, the greatest trainer I've ever had the privilege of knowing. A horse trainer is a very big deal in racing. Kind of like a college football coach, the trainer has a team of horses and he decides when to run them, which races to put them in, and what jockeys to put on them. Frankie Brothers was a top trainer who had horses that could run.

So he pretty much had his pick of any of the best jockeys in Chicago.

Frankie and I met at Arlington Park and at first I was very intimidated by him. He was so well respected that I almost didn't know how to act around him. But the more I rode for him, the more I realized that there was nothing to be nervous about. Frankie was a genuinely wonderful guy and he deserved every bit of respect he got.

Not only was Frankie one of the rare trainers who treated jockeys well, but he also had his horses' best interest in mind. Everything about Frankie was great. I went through my life looking for a father figure that I could look up to and Frankie was that father figure. Whenever he spoke to me, I always answered him with a "Yes Sir" or a "No Sir" because I wanted to please him. Just like my dad, I wanted to please Frankie.

And even though he never said it, I knew I did please him. Frankie didn't have any kids and I could tell that he cared about me almost the way a father should care about a son. We had a mutual respect and admiration for each other and I know he will always be as special to me as I hope I was to him.

I don't know if I ever actually said this to him, but Frankie was the biggest part of my success. He believed in me and made me believe in myself. He understood me, even when I got hotheaded, and he was always there to make me feel better. That, in turn, made me ride better and it made me feel like I wasn't mentally fatherless.

The more time I spent with Frankie and the other jocks, the more I realized how much family meant. And given the state of my biological family, I knew that I was ready to have a family of my own.

About a month after Kelli moved to Chicago, I took her to my friend John Saban's nice restaurant called Saban's. While we walked down the tiled floor to our seats, Kelli didn't realize that I had more than dinner on my mind. However, when she reached for her wine glass and found a diamond ring glimmering at the bottom, my intentions became pretty obvious.

I remember my heart racing and my hands shaking as I reached out to take Kelli's hand in my own. With the excitement of a little boy in a candy shop, I gently held her hand and asked, "Kelli, will you marry me?"

I'll never forget her beautiful smile when she looked at the ring, looked at me, and said, "Yes! Yes, I'll marry you!"

That was one of the happiest moments of my life. Kelli and I spent the rest of the night dancing on the wooden dance floor, kissing, and whispering loving thoughts in each other's ears. Between her natural beauty and her excitement, Kelli glowed like a golden goddess. We were in love and I'm sure that everybody at Saban's that night knew it.

When we went back to our place, Kelli and I kissed like we were teenagers and we just couldn't get enough of each other's lips. We stayed like that until morning and for the first time in my life, I felt like I was truly home.

That's how things were with us every night from that point on. Sure, we had some ups and downs like all couples do, but for the most part, our relationship was magical. While I hung out with Robby, Mike, and Kerwin, I could still feel the good from Kelli radiating through my pores. She made me a better friend; she made me a better jockey; she made me a better man. Kelli completed me and made me whole.

With those thoughts in mind, Kelli and I got married as quickly as we possibly could. We exchanged our vows and had our reception at Saban's because that seemed to be the most appropriate place for us to make our union official. We had a small wedding, but it was perfect nonetheless.

All of my jockey friends came and they were the only family I had there. My parents didn't come, my brothers didn't come, and my sister didn't come. That didn't matter, though, because I had my self-made family to witness the new family that Kelli and I were forming.

It was also terrific that Kelli's mother Maxine was there to support us. She was thrilled for both of us and her face gleamed with happiness all night long. She got right out there on the dance floor with all of us, partying and dancing the night away. That night I got a second mother and I couldn't have been prouder to call Maxine "Mom."

During that period of my life, it was like the rest of the world knew how complete my life was and that they wanted to make it even more perfect. That point was proven when a horse named Fighting Fantasy was sent from Kentucky to Chicago. I won a race on him at Sportsman's Park and the impossible happened: they wanted me to ride him in the Kentucky Derby!

When I heard the good news, I think my heart stopped beating. Did I want to ride in the Kentucky Derby? Of course I did! That is every jockey's dream and up until that moment I never expected that dream to come true. By that time I had learned the difference between a skilled horse and a phenomenal one, and I knew that Fighting Fantasy fit into the first category. I knew I didn't even stand a chance to win the Derby, but that didn't matter. The point was that I was going to ride with the greatest riders in the greatest race in America!

When Derby time came, Kelli and I went to Louisville, unsure of what to expect. What we saw was more than we could have even imagined. Being a jockey in the Kentucky Derby is a bit like standing outside Willie Wonka's gate with a golden ticket in your hand. People immediately took notice and started waving, blowing kisses, and hooting and hollering. Even though I didn't have a huge name at the time, I felt like a celebrity.

Churchill Downs was so packed for the big day that I think the crowd would have outnumbered the population of Erath, Lockport, and the whole state of Louisiana, combined. Derby Day was like a combination of a festival, a circus, and a trip to Hollywood, all in one. Celebrities sat in their special boxes, women sat on the edge of their seats with their big hats framing their perfectly made-up faces, and jockeys' families sat with their fingers crossed, hoping for the absolute best. The enthusiasm in the air was intoxicating and I felt even more excited than I did all those years ago when I saw my first Derby on TV with my father.

When the time finally came, I mounted Fighting Fantasy and minutes later sent him into his stall in the starting gate. I didn't feel any pressure because I didn't expect to win. The horse was the longest long shot in the race at odds of 111-1. But all I felt was excitement to be at Churchill Downs in the presence of the country's most talented jockeys for the most anticipated race in the world.

It seemed like hours went by while we waited in the starting gate for all 15 horses to be loaded. All I could see was the crowd and I could hear it getting louder and louder as each horse got in. I kept a tight hold on the reins as I waited for the gate to spring open for the start of the Kentucky Derby. When it finally did, Fighting Fantasy was off and he was off at a fast gallop. That horse had speed, but I could tell he felt sore. He was trying to bear out, but he did get the lead. Around the first, though, Fighting Fantasy went really wide. Trying to salvage my position in the race, I got him back over with the leaders as we turned onto the backstretch, but he faded after that and finished last. That was okay. I never really expected to win, but I was already a winner in my mind just for being there. That was my first of many Derbies, and I wouldn't have had it any other way.

When the excitement of the Derby finally wore off and Kelli and I retreated from all of the after parties and celebrations, it was time to get back to life as we knew it. For some people, that might sound boring. But our life was so wonderful at that time that we were happy to go back to Chicago together.

When we got back, things went on as they always did. I rode in as many races as I could and I kept my position as leading rider. That was a big deal with so many excellent riders around. I hung around with Mike, Mark, Robby, and Kerwin, joking around and laughing like I used to with C.D. and Breezy. Most importantly, I spent as much time with Kelli as I could – and our time together showed when Kelli found out she was pregnant.

I'll always remember the feeling of pride and love I experienced when Kelli told me the news. We were going to be parents; I was going to be a daddy! I vowed to myself right then and there that we were going to do this right. I would never treat Kelli like my dad treated my mom and I would never treat our child like my father treated me. We were going to have a good, loving family, just as God intended it.

Kelli's pregnancy went by quickly, though it was probably faster for me than it was for her. I stayed by her side as much as I could, but I also had to stick to my racing schedule. By that time, the races had swung over to Arlington Park, and I was pretty busy.

I loved my time at Arlington, though, because like Sportsman's Park, it brought along more friends. I became really good friends with Randy Romero and he became like another one of my brothers. He was from Erath, too, and I always looked up to him as a kid. It was great to have such a great support network both on the track, in the box, and at home.

On one particular day at Arlington I had several mounts to ride, when I got a phone call in the jocks' room. When I picked up the phone, the last thing I expected to hear was that Kelli was in labor! I immediately took off all my mounts and headed to the hospital with my brain flying in a million different directions.

I've always loved kids and babies. To have one of my own with someone I truly loved was the most special thing I could imagine. When I got to Kelli's hospital room, I put on the daddy gown and tried to help her with her Lamaze exercises. I held onto her hand and tried to pretend that she didn't hurt me when the pain became too much and she squeezed the hell out of it.

As a racing fan, through and through, I couldn't resist the temptation to tune the TV in her room to the Arlington Million. While Kelli breathed in and out, in and out, I kept turning my head from her reddened face to the TV screen. When it got to the point where I felt like Kelli was going to rip my hand right off, either from her pain or from her annoyance of me watching TV while she went through the most painful experience of her life, I pretended that the TV didn't even exist. Our baby was coming and that was all that mattered.

After more breathing and crying and screaming, the doctor finally announced that our baby had a head. I didn't know all that much about childbirth, so I thought that was a pretty good sign.

Then little by little, our baby popped out further and further as Kelli kept pushing and squeezing my hand for dear life.

Then it finally happened. Kelli's long labor was over and we had the most beautiful baby girl I had ever seen. Staring at our gorgeous baby like I was seeing a miracle, I couldn't believe that she was a part of me; that she was a part of us. That was the most special feeling in the world.

After I cut the umbilical cord and the nurses cleaned her up, I put my arm around Kelli while she held our baby girl. In a near whisper, I said, "She's the best part of both of us." And when I asked Kelli what we were going to name our new baby girl, she confirmed my statement with her suggestion.

The combination of the first three letters of my name and the last two letters of Kelli's name symbolized our roles in our new daughter's life. Still holding onto one another, we welcomed our beautiful Shali into the world.

Chapter 11

Once I became a daddy, time flew by faster than it ever had before. Shali became my little princess and Kelli and I grew closer every day that we spent with our gorgeous little girl. Something about a baby smiling up at you while she sticks her big toe in her mouth puts life into perspective and makes every moment seem precious.

Those precious moments go by fast, though. Shali started off as a gurgling baby, but soon she could crawl away at a moment's notice and hide like a CIA operative. Then she became a running toddler who could run around our place faster than I used to run through the streets in Erath. And finally, she became a three-year-old with a big responsibility – being a big sister.

In 1993, Kelli gave birth to our second child. Thankfully this labor didn't last nearly as long as the first and at the end we had a healthy baby boy. I couldn't believe it; I had my very own son. Now I had two beautiful children and I knew that I was going to love them like no father ever loved a child before. They wouldn't have to hide in the doorways crying like I did when I was a kid and they would never have to wonder if daddy truly loved them. Everything was going to be perfect for them and I would make sure of that until my last dying breath.

Kelli and I knew right away what we should name our baby boy. Just like Shali was made from pieces of us, our son was a reflection of our love. So when the time came to give him a name, nothing seemed more appropriate than Saban, the name of the place where we got engaged and had our wedding. To this day, every time I say my son's name, I remember the love and happiness that Kelli and I have shared throughout our relationship.

Of course, our relationship has come with many ups and downs as any relationship does. By the time Saban was born, I was really building a name for myself in the racing world and I had to spend a lot of time away from my family. I still primarily rode in Chicago, but now I had to travel to other states, as well, to ride in bigger races.

For instance, in 1995, I flew to Oklahoma City to ride in the Silver Bullet Stakes. At that point, I had ridden and won quite a few big races like the American Derby at Arlington Park and the Ashland Stakes at Keeneland Race Course, in the heart of Kentucky horse country. But this was one race that I particularly wanted to win.

On the day of the race, I met a man named Barry Golden who owned the horse I was going to ride. I already knew what a good horse Golden Gear was, but I was surprised to see that Barry was just as great. We must have spent an hour talking before the race and this was not like the usual pep talks that most owners give. Barry was a very nice and down-to-earth guy who I genuinely enjoyed spending time with. By the time we finished chatting before the race, I knew I had to win – not just for me, but for him.

As I sat on Golden Gear, ready to break from the gate, I thought my determination alone would help us win the race. When the gates opened, we broke well and Golden Gear was off and running. That horse knew what he was doing and I barely had to guide him. It was like he wanted to win for Barry as much as I did. With both of our minds set on the same goal, Golden Gear and I hit the finish line so fast that some of the other horses may have still been standing at the gate. He ran one of his most impressive races, setting a track record and placing all of our names in Remington Park history.

After the race and the winner's circle photo, I jumped off the horse with my heart still pounding from the thrill of the race. I was so happy that my face almost hurt from smiling so much. Barry was just as excited as I was and I was proud that I'd won this for him.

Apparently my first instincts about Barry were right because our relationship didn't end after our picture was taken. Barry stayed in touch with me and remains one of my nearest and dearest friends to this day.

That is just one example of a time I had to travel to ride a horse, but sometimes I had to travel to race in other ways, too. In the same year, I went to Saratoga, the famous New York track, for a very unusual Jockey Challenge. Unlike most of our challenge competitions, this one pit jockey against jockey without any horses! I know it sounds odd, but that was one of the greatest races of my life.

Before the race began, the jockeys and I sat around egging each other on. I particularly remember talking with my friends

Frankie Lovato, Jerry Bailey, and Jose Martinez, poking fun at them just as much as they poked fun at me. Between the four of us, a flurry of good humored insults floated around the open air.

"So, are you ready to lose, my man?"

"Let's see how good you race without one of your fancy horses under you."

"Good luck because you're all going to need it!"

"See you losers at the finish line."

We all laughed good naturedly and wished each other luck. Then all of us jockeys took our post positions in the starting gate. I cannot even describe how weird it felt to be in the gate without a horse.

Before the start, I tried to come up with the best strategy. I figured that my best chance would be to zoom out of the gate and get a head start before anybody knew what was coming. So I lunged my left leg forward with my bare toes stuck in the dirt and my head firmly plastered against the gate. My nose smooshed into the padded door and I stood like that until the gate opened. When it finally did, I practically fell out of the gate, running like I was a kid again.

I took off like a bullet and vaguely saw Jerry fall flat on his face at the start of the race. Trying not to laugh, I kept running and for a while, it looked like I was going to win. At the last second, John Velasquez and Filiberto Leon nipped me at the wire. Filiberto won in a photo finish with me trailing right behind him and John.

When that race ended, I laughed harder than I had ever laughed before. Jerry scooped himself up from the dirt and came over to join all of us in the winners circle for a victory photo. We all stood together smiling and laughing, happy to participate in such a fun and crazy race with each other.

Even though I came in third on that race, it felt like we were all winners. That was one of the strangest and best moments I had as a jockey. And as sure as I'm smiling now as I think back on it, I think I smiled the whole way home.

When I got back home to my family's new home in Kentucky, I was still smiling just as brightly. Looking back, I had every reason to smile. Not only had I run in the "big" race and returned to my family, but we had another family member on the way. That's right – Kelli was pregnant again!

In 1996, Kelli brought another little girl into the world. This time her labor went by so quickly that it seemed like she was becoming a pro at this. I still held onto her hand and helped her with her breathing – but this time I had learned my lesson and I didn't watch the TV in between breaths. Before long, our new baby's head came out and then her shoulders and then her perfect little feet. We may have gone through these motions three times already, but I was as excited and proud as I was when Shali was born. Just like the births of our first two children, I held onto Kelli and cried out of joy. Our family was complete and it was perfect.

This time when we named our baby girl, we did things a bit differently. We were friends with a jockey named Joe Steiner who rode in Chicago. Kelli thought his last name was really neat, so we named our baby Steiner. Now we had three children who represented all aspects of our lives: our love, our marriage, and our equal passion for horse racing. All in all, we seemed to have everything we could hope for.

The best part was that I was able to bring my best friends into our family even more than they were before. All of our children were christened by jockeys and that only brought us closer together. Kerwin Clark became Shali's godfather, Mark Guidry and his wife Tina became Saban's godparents, and Mike Smith and his wife Patrice became Steiner's godparents. If we couldn't all be considered as family before, we sure could now.

So now my life was divided into two equal parts: my family and my career. My family was obviously more important to me than anything else, but my career was very high up on my scale of priorities. Fortunately, I still rode a lot in Chicago, so it wasn't all that difficult to balance the two main categories of my life.

I won a lot of races in Chicago, but the most important for me was the 1996 Secretariat Stakes at Arlington Park. The race was one and a quarter miles on Arlington's famous grass course. The Secretariat carried a $500,000 purse and horses shipped in from all over to compete. There were even some horses from overseas.

I was a leading rider at that time and Wayne Lukas had named me to ride his horse, Marlin. Wayne was the leading trainer in the country and he was setting all kinds of records for the money his horses earned. It seemed like the perfect combination and I couldn't have been happier.

I admit that I was nervous to ride for Mr. Lukas because his reputation spread far and wide – and I'm not just talking about his reputation for winning. In the jocks' room, a lot of people had things to say about Wayne and not all of them were good. I heard that he was a horse butcher and a jockey's worst nightmare. But still, Wayne must have done something right because there was no way to deny how many wins his horses were piling up.

When the time came, I met with Mr. Lukas and we talked about Marlin, the horse I would be riding. Talking with him before the race was nothing like talking to Barry Golden. Wayne was very upfront about his expectations and he wanted to lay all my moves out for me. That was a very strange situation because there is really no way to anticipate what you are going to do until you get on the horse and ride. It's easy to say that you'll ride the rail and stay tight on the turns, but it doesn't always work out that way. You have to figure in the horses that are beside you, behind you, and in front of you. After all, a horse collision isn't going to help anybody, so the only way to ride properly is to play the race by ear.

Still, Mr. Lukas had a game plan and he wanted me to stick to it. I tried to be respectful and I told him I would do my best to stick with his strategy, but I got the feeling that my best wouldn't be good enough unless I came in first.

Walking away from our meeting, I was more than a little bit nervous about the race. But I had confidence in myself and I knew that Marlin had a great chance of winning.

As we approached the starting gate, I tried to remember everything that Wayne had said. I didn't want to disappoint him, but I also didn't want to ride like I was following a basketball play written on a chalkboard. So when those gates opened, I did what I did best: I came up with my own strategy as I rode and I let that strategy lead me to victory.

When Marlin and I barreled across the finish line first, I couldn't believe my luck. This was undoubtedly the biggest race of my career and I won it easily. Not only did I win that very important race, but I shattered Randy Romero's impressive record of 182 wins in a year by winning 218 races. The doors to my future were now open and I knew that fantastic things were going to come.

Chapter 12

By the time 1997 rolled around, I was one of the leading riders in the country and it seemed like my career would go on forever. My closest friends were also my biggest competitors and I loved that fact. People like Mark Guidry and Jerry Bailey motivated me to be a better rider and I think I did the same for them. We may have been warriors on the track, but we were brothers in the jocks' room.

With over 3,000 victories under my belt, I was making great money and living life like a rock star. If Kelli wanted something, she got it. If my kids wanted something, I would give them two. I was very generous with my money and I never really thought anything of handing it out. After growing up in Erath, I knew what it was like to be poor, so I was happy to share my winnings with all of my loved ones.

As time went on, though, I started to realize that not many jockeys were as fortunate as I was. The majority of the jockeys in the country were still working for $50 per mount and in some cases, they actually had to pay to ride.

For instance, let's talk about the Kentucky Derby. If you're lucky enough to win that race, you'll practically be able to live forever off your winnings. But if you place anywhere from fourth to last, you have to pay for your family's tickets plus travel expenses to claim your $100 check – and that's not counting the taxes you have to pay on the $100. Then you have to pay your agent, your valet, and Uncle Sam. At the end, you'll be lucky to go home with $60.

It doesn't take a rocket scientist to figure out that something is wrong here. I had to pay $1,000 for each Derby so I could get tickets for Kelli and the kids. Four people would go home with money and 17 other riders go home with around $940 less than they started with. That's a pretty extreme example, but it's a valid one, nonetheless.

The same rules apply to ordinary, day-to-day races. Every jocks' room is filled with countless jockeys who are struggling just to get by. Like me, a lot of them never finished school so they didn't know what else they could do with their lives. Lacking a proper education and unable to get mounts on good horses because of their riding stats, these jockeys busted their asses riding bad horses just to try and get food on the table.

Considering the other major bodies of sports, that seemed more than unfair. You could be the worst football player on a team and still make six figures a year. You could be a rookie pro wrestler and still have plenty of money for a house and a new car. You could even be the slowest racecar driver on the track and still make tons of money by plastering so many endorsements on your body that you looked like a walking billboard.

But jockeys? We were only worth $50 per mount.

Clearly that system was wrong and we wanted to do something to make it right. If racecar drivers and other athletes could wear product endorsements, why couldn't we? It only seemed fair that we should get the opportunity to make a decent amount of money for risking our lives to put on a show for the crowd. Even if it wasn't much, at least it would be better than an insulting $50. Plus, we would be bringing corporate America into the game of horse racing, thus helping everyone in the industry.

So in 1997, I decided to take that theory and put it into action. I was getting ready to ride Skip Away in the MassCap, and that seemed like the perfect opportunity to make a serious change in the industry. My agent spoke to the powers at Suffolk Downs and then he spoke to a steward on the track. Since nobody could find a good reason for jockeys *not* to wear endorsements, Suffolk Downs and I made history in the '97 MassCap.

For the first time ever, a jockey was allowed to wear a patch with a product endorsement on his leg for a bit of extra cash. Suffolk Downs will always hold a special place in my heart for allowing that to happen. Although that particular race only had one jockey with one patch, their kindness allowed me to pave the way for the future.

When the day of the race came, I was as excited as I was nervous. I brandished my Breathe Right patch proudly, eager to show it off as much as possible. But I knew I was making history that day, so I knew I had to put on a great show for all of the eyes that would be on me and my endorsed leg.

On the day of the race, I knew I was in for some very stiff competition, but all I could do was try my hardest and hope for the best. I had a good feeling that Skip Away would turn in a top effort as he always did, so our chances were pretty great.

I kept that thought in mind while I waited in the starting gate. I could hear the crowd hooting and hollering, cheering on their favorite horses. Skip Away had lost his last four races, but I still had faith in him. He may not have been as lucky as the infamous Cigar was in his last few races, but he was still an outstanding horse. An *outstanding* horse.

Gripping the reins, I felt confident, but it felt like centuries passed while I waited for the gate to open. When it finally did open, Skip Away and I were both ready. We careened out of the gate, galloping at a fierce speed. At first, it looked like it could be anybody's game. But when we rounded the turn and went for home, we got up at the wire to beat Formal Gold in a photo finish.

That was one of the proudest moments of my career. Not only did Skip Away come back in high style, and not only did Suffolk Downs let me wear a patch on my pants, but we made New England headlines for Skip Away earning $500,000 for winning the MassCap, with the entire day at Suffolk Downs carrying a record million dollars in purses. To put things lightly, I was on top of the world.

Afterwards, I left Boston with illusions of grandeur. If Massachusetts could be so kind as to let me wear an endorsement patch, how many other places would follow suit? How many jockeys could break away from poverty and live better lifestyles?

How many lives could be improved by one simple action in one simple race?

At the time, the possibilities seemed endless. For the first time in many years, I wasn't just looking at things from a leading rider's perspective. I was looking out for every jockey who deserved better.

Soon after the MassCap, I decided that I would use every power I had as a regional director of the Jockey's Guild. My peers voted for me to take that position in 1990 and now I was ready to use my power to its full advantage. Now I would have the chance to really make a difference and to be the voice for all the jockeys who couldn't – or wouldn't – speak for themselves. I would be able to take action on concerns that bothered riders regionally and take those concerns to the annual Jockey's Guild national meetings. I would go to the yearly meetings, speak on behalf of my comrades, and truly make a difference in their lives.

For the first time ever, I wasn't just looking out for me and my family; I was looking out for *all* the riders.

And at that time, I truly thought the riders would look out for me, too.

Chapter 13

I always thought the more I advanced in my career, the better a man I would become. As time proved, my theory was wrong.

It's not like I became my father or anything like that. I just found myself feeling angrier than I used to. A lot of jockeys thought I was hotheaded, but that wasn't really the case. I was raised to speak up for what I believe in; to stand up and fight for myself. My dad wouldn't have let me sit quietly in the corner – unless it came to dealing with him – so I verbalized every qualm I had throughout my career.

If one of my fellow jockeys did something that I didn't like, I told him. I wasn't trying to be a jerk; I was standing up for what I believed in. When a confrontation broke out in the jocks' room, it was usually easy to solve. But when a confrontation broke out because of a trainer or an owner, things were not so easy.

What most people don't realize is that horse racing is not just a game; it's a political battle. If you want to get anywhere, you have to bite your tongue, even when you know you're right. You have to say "Yes Sir" and "No Sir" to every person who degrades you and makes you feel like you're nothing. You have to keep a smile on your face, even when you're being cussed out. No matter how rude or arrogant or mean someone is to you, you have to act like you're in the presence of a King.

Well, I might have been a big part of the Sport of Kings, but I wasn't about to bow down to anybody. As time went on and I saw what a political battle it was to stay in good graces, I knew a war was inevitable.

My crusade started one day when I was riding for Wayne Lukas. At this point in my career, it was a well-known fact that Wayne and I didn't get along very well. He was demeaning to jockeys and even though everyone was sugar sweet to his face, the grumbles started as soon as they got back to the jocks' room. I was probably one of the leading grumblers, but I wasn't afraid to say my thoughts to his face, either.

Right before the 1998 Florida Derby, I was riding on a talented horse named Cape Town for Wayne. Cape Town was a top prospect for the Kentucky Derby. He was also a top prospect for the Florida Derby in March at Gulfstream Park in Miami, which was the richest prep race along the trail to the Kentucky Derby and the Triple Crown. The racing world is focused on the prep races for the Kentucky Derby, and the press follows the moves of all the top contenders. It's an exciting time in racing, and to be on a horse like Cape Town, with a chance at winning the Derby, is the greatest feeling of anticipation a jock can have.

For me, the chance to ride in the Florida Derby had a lot of meaning that had nothing to do with the honor behind the Derby itself. Out of all the racetracks I ever rode at, Gulfstream Park was one of the best. The people who worked there were fantastic, the crowds were very excited, and the atmosphere was as comfortable as it was fun. So for me, the 1998 Florida Derby was extra special because I genuinely wanted to participate in such a fun race at such a great location.

One morning I got on the horse, adjusted my saddle, and got ready to breeze him. While I was getting ready, Wayne's assistant Jerry Barton came up to me on his pony and said, "Hey Coach!"

Normally when Jerry spoke to me, he was very chipper. But that day he sounded like he had just been through the worst experience of his life. I asked him, "What's wrong? Have a bad night?"

Jerry took a deep breath and responded, "Shane, look. I know how you are, but Wayne told me this horse is probably gonna get out with you. The vet is here from California. But whatever you do, don't tell the vet the horse is getting out. He'll be fine by Saturday."

Wayne's message didn't seem like so much of a request as a demand. I didn't want to lie to the vet or put the horse in danger, but I figured that I would take good care of Cape Town. After all, Wayne said that he would be fine by Saturday, so I believed him.

Feeling extremely uncomfortable, I rode Cape Town down to the half pole and then galloped him back. I could tell that he was sore so I tried to take the best care of him that I could. All the while, I knew the vet was watching from the quarter pole in the observation room. When I jumped off the horse and greeted the vet, I was so appalled by the lie I was about to tell that I couldn't

116

even manage to stay in his presence. I had never lied to a vet before and I didn't want to start now. But it didn't seem like I had much of a choice, so when the vet asked me how Cape Town went, I reluctantly said, "I gotta get on another horse, doc, but he went well and he'll do great on Saturday." Then I just walked away because I didn't know what else to do.

On the day of the Florida Derby, I could see that Cape Town was not nearly as fine as Wayne promised he would be. He felt a bit better than he had a few days before, but he wasn't in great shape. His pain wasn't visible to others, but I could tell he was sore.

To make matters worse, it rained that day, so the ground was slicker than usual. Right at post time, the wind really whipped up; it began to rain and the sky got very dark. I tried to stay down on my horse to make it easier on him, and I don't think I used my stick on him once. The race was amazing. Cape Town came from behind and caught Lil's Lad right at the wire. Lil's Lad won the photo by just a nose, but the horse was disqualified for coming out into us just before the finish and certainly costing Cape Town the chance the win the race outright. The stewards reversed the order of finish and Cape Town was named the official winner of the Florida Derby. He sure deserved it.

After winning a race with that kind of prestige, it's hard to just walk away from a horse. People would have thought I was crazy. I figured that they could either put him in the Bluegrass or in the Kentucky Derby, but certainly not in both. However, I was wrong. Cape Town was entered next in the Bluegrass Stakes at

Keeneland as his final prep for the Kentucky Derby. And I was named to ride.

There were just five horses in the Bluegrass, but we started from the outside post and even in that small a field, we couldn't get over to the rail. Jerry Bailey was riding Lil's Lad, who was again the big favorite in the betting. Lil's Lad broke well and grabbed the rail. Jerry saw what was going on and I could see him crouching down with his head on top of his horse, slowing down the pace of the race. Bailey, being the great rider he was, had his horse's head cocked over the fence, protecting the rail. I was the only one near him, and I knew he wasn't going to get off the fence if I didn't press him. Wayne wanted me to stay on the fence, but my horse was getting out. So I started to pick up the pace as we went into the turn. We turned for home and Cape Town gave it his all, but we came in third. Halory Hunter, with Gary Stevens riding, came on and passed both Jerry and me to get the win.

At that point, I was hardly concerned about not winning the race. All I knew was that Cape Town was done running. I knew it, he knew it, and I'm certain that Wayne knew it. But when the race was over, Wayne had the gall to dog me out in front of all the fans and the jockeys. He blamed the loss on me and started telling everyone – including the press – that I rode his horse badly and cost Cape Town the race. The press butchered me for that and I looked like the asshole because the words came out of the mighty Mr. Lukas' mouth.

Feeling absolutely furious, the next morning I walked into Wayne's tack room and confronted him about what had happened. I said, "Why can't you come back to me and take me into this office and tell me what you gotta say? Why do you gotta go and hurt me in the press when you know it's the total opposite, Wayne? You knew that horse was lame before the Florida Derby and you run him in the Bluegrass. Then he runs bad and you blame me"

Getting angrier by the second, I continued, "What a scapegoat. You just bounced it off on me and it's wrong. Take your horses. I don't need to ride for you, man. You understand? I don't. I'm gonna win races without you cause you haven't even put me on too many winners, man. How many winners have you put me on?"

In a final fit of anger, I said, "I've made it this far without you and to be honest with you, I don't respect you as a person or as a horseman. The way you treated this horse, they should take away your license. He didn't belong in the Bluegrass, much less the Derby. You knew it before the Florida Derby and that's why you told me he was gonna get out and not to tell the vet." Then I walked out of his office and never walked back.

Wayne didn't say anything to me at the time, but his actions showed what he thought of my words when he put Jerry Bailey on Cape Town in the '98 Kentucky Derby. I knew that horse was done after his last race and I couldn't believe that Wayne was going to put him in another. Not only was that dangerous for Cape Town, but it was dangerous for Jerry and every other jockey on that track.

I went to Jerry on Derby Day and said, "Jerry, man, don't think you picked up a 5-to-1 shot that's got a chance. In fact, be careful." He looked at me and I said, "I worked him before the Florida Derby and this horse was already going bad at that point. Then I rode him in the Florida Derby and in the Blue Grass. Wayne told me not to tell anybody, but go back to the Derby and look at it; look at its knees." Jerry thanked me for the heads up and then we were off to ride in yet another Derby.

When we got onto the track, Jerry saw how right I was. He pulled Cape Town up and finished the race, but he finished 30 lengths back. Jerry pulled him off and that was Cape Town's last race. Now he's a stallion and he'll never race again.

The fact that Cape Town made it through the Kentucky Derby is irrelevant. What if he broke down during that race? He would have been completely crippled. The crowd would have sat there watching one of their favorite horses, oblivious to what was happening when the big green tarp went up in front of him. Then, just like it happens to so many other crippled horses, the vets would try to save him. If they couldn't, they would have hidden the horse behind the tarp while they gave him a shot, put a chain around his neck, and hauled his dead body into one of the horse ambulances that wait in limbo at every single race.

I know things like that are bound to happen in horse racing, but that's not the point. Just like jockeys put their lives on the line, horses do the same. But when the odds show that a horse probably won't make it, that takes things too far. That takes horse racing from a game to a slaughter house.

And that's the problem with men like Wayne Lukas. The public views him as a hero, but we jockeys know better. Sure, we wanted to get on his horses because he bought the best bred horses in the country. Since the best-bred horses usually make the best racehorses, it's obvious that he should have won as many races as he did. But instead of treating his horses right and letting them have lengthy careers, history shows that Wayne's horses were lucky if they made it past three-year-old years. He pushed them until they broke down.

Everyone in the jocks' room knew that, but they sure wouldn't say it – not to Wayne's face, anyway. In jockey politics, everyone treated Wayne like he was a god and then walked back into the jocks' room talking about what a jerk he was. We knew how his horses felt because that was our job. We could feel the struggle in their knees and the jolts in their backs. We could see their eyes widen when we got on them, as if they were saying "Why are you doing this to me?" We could see all of it, but there was nobody there to listen to our side of the story.

So we sat around and watched as the best bred horses in the country broke down, one after another. Wayne kept winning races, but what happened to the horses after the race? That man became an all-time legend, but he lacked the compassion to be great in the long-term. If you look for Wayne Lukas' winning horses now, you can't find them with a search warrant.

Wayne didn't forget how to train; he just can't get the same kind of horses that he used to. His statistics show that his horses either won big or lost big. There was no in between. He had the opportunity to work with the best, most expensive horses; he just didn't treat them well enough for them to prosper like they could have.

But that's just another part of the bullshit jockey politics that nobody knows – or wants to know – about. Horses and jockeys are nothing more than property; expensive or really cheap property. If we don't stick up for ourselves, nobody will. We're just bug boys and no boys, two terms that are used in the racing world quite frequently.

This political nonsense really got to me and it started to show in my day-to-day life. I was so angry at people like Wayne that I unwillingly started to become like them. Believe me, that was the last thing I wanted, but it was an instinct that I just couldn't help. My anger and animosity overpowered me, and soon almost everyone could feel my wrath.

I could feel myself acting short with my wife and with my fellow jockeys. I didn't want to argue with them and I knew that on some level. But I was just so angry that I couldn't help myself. I needed to take out my anger on someone, and unfortunately, that someone just happened to be in the wrong place at the wrong time.

One day I was riding for a man whose name I can't even remember. He didn't have many horses and the horses he did have didn't look good on paper. I had nine horses to ride that day and this was the sixth one I rode in a row.

I don't know how much weight I had pulled that day, but I was starving; I was weak like a wet noodle. My head was spinning and my legs could hardly move. I felt like I was dying and I still had three more horses to ride that day.

So there I was, getting ready to mount a horse whose odds were something like 25-to-1. I was mad at my agent for putting me on this horse to begin with, especially considering how many other horses I had to deal with that day. I asked my agent, "Can't you call this guy and ask him to take me off and let another one of your jockeys ride it, instead? I already have nine horses in a row, man."

So when I went in to meet the owner, I was already mad. I was aggravated about my starvation, my dizziness, my long day, and everything that was still on my mind because of Wayne. Simply put, I was really pissed off that day and I shouldn't have been around anyone.

Still, it wasn't the owner's fault, so I said "hello" and tried to be really nice to him. They legged me up and I could barely get my feet in the irons. It looked like the horse didn't want to be with me any more than I wanted to be with him because he was throwing his head and slinging himself around.

By the time I got to the track, I was fuming. The horse kept trying to sling me off and throw me around. When we broke from the gate, we went about a quarter of a mile and the horse just stopped. From that point on, he kept stopping and starting, and it was the longest ride ever to get him through his last turn for home.

When the race finally ended, I pulled him up and galloped him home. His trainer grabbed the horse, still shaking his head, and said, "Shane, I'm sorry. Just get off."

So I got off and my feet hit the ground. When the horse stepped away, he stepped right on top of my foot. And out of all the times in the world this horse could have picked, he wouldn't get off my foot when I tried to push him away. Instead, he just leaned back and relaxed while the weight of his body crushed my foot beneath my thin boot.

When he finally got off of me, I was furious. I don't know what came over me. A combination of anger, starvation, and exhaustion took me over and I wasn't myself anymore. Without even knowing what I was about to do, I reached back and kicked the horse underneath the belly.

The moment my foot made contact with him, I knew that I was acting out of control. I wished I could take my action back or pretend it never happened, but I couldn't. The crowd was right there, watching me over the fence, and the kind-hearted trainer was right there, too. The horse started running in circles and I knew I had screwed things up beyond repair. So struck by fear, shame, and anger, I grabbed all of my things and walked away.

Rightly, the owner must have said something to my agent because he turned me into the stewards. They fined me, justly so, because I should have known better. I love horses like they're people and I would never want to hurt one. But on that particular day at that particular moment, I was like a different man – and a very bad one at that.

After that incident, I knew that something needed to change; not only inside of me, but inside of the industry itself. I was acting like someone I wasn't and it wasn't just because of a bad mood. All of the downfalls of the industry were starting to catch up with me and I just couldn't handle things the way I used to.

The only way to change things in this industry is from the inside out. I knew I would have to go through a lot of mean trainers, stewards, clerks of scales, and yes, even stubborn asses like Shane Sellers, but I was ready to fight. If I couldn't do things the fair way – the right way – I would find another way to make sure that there would be no more stories like Cape Town's; that there would be no more disgruntled jockeys.

My daddy raised me to be a fighter, and as far as I was concerned, the games were on.

Chapter 14

When I first moved to Kentucky in the mid-90s, I had one intention in mind: Go to Churchill Downs and dethrone Pat Day, the leading rider. I certainly had nothing against Pat as a person or as a jockey, but he was the king of Churchill Downs and taking that title for myself was my next step in advancing my career. If you can make it as leading rider at Churchill Downs, you can do just about anything – especially since Pat Day had been leading rider since the 1980s.

Looking back, sometimes I think that's where I went wrong. You can see the tension of horse racing politics on every track in the country. But at Churchill Downs, you more than *see* it; you can feel it crackling in the air.

Despite the overwhelming political games, I achieved my goal. I beat Pat Day and became leading rider at what is quite possibly the most famous racetrack in the world. That was when some of the top trainers around the country wanted to give me an opportunity and that was also when I realized that victory has as much to do with the horse as with the jockey. You can put a great jockey on a bad horse and he'll probably lose. But if you put a bad jockey on a great horse, he'll probably win.

Of course, that's not the case every time. Horse racing is a team sport and you need the jockey and the horse, as well as the owners and trainers and grooms and hot walkers – everybody in the stable who works to get good horses ready to race. Everybody has to work together for it to succeed. When you can't get everyone to work together, though, you might as well strap a monkey to a horse's back because nobody can get very far with a good, but crippled horse.

After the incident with Cape Town, I saw Wayne Lukas every single day and neither of us ever said a word to each other. We would walk by each other pretending that there was nothing but air and grass surrounding us. Then we would continue on our separate ways.

But one day something changed. I was walking past Wayne like I always did, when all of a sudden he yelled out, "Hey Coach!"

I wanted to keep walking, but my agent said, "Come on Shane." So I went up to Wayne to see what he could possibly want from me.

Gritting my teeth and forcing my best political smile, I stood next to Wayne and said, "Hey, how ya doin?"

Wayne said to me, "You know, you're gonna win races without me and I'm gonna win races without you. But if we get together, we'll win a lot more races."

I couldn't believe my ears. After all he did to me a year ago, he would actually suggest that we should work together again?

Flabbergasted, I responded to Wayne, "Well, I can't ride for you Mr. Wayne cause you're not gonna treat me like that. I'm not gonna allow you to treat me like that. If I'm wrong, fine. And am I gonna make mistakes? Yes I am. But to do that to me in public?

No. To humiliate me? No. And you were wrong. You were *wrong*! You knew that horse was lame."

I spent a long time feeling livid; hating the very idea of Wayne's suggestion. Even thinking about it now makes my blood boil. But as much as I wanted to stay away from the politics and as much as I wanted to stay away from horse racing's greatest politician, I eventually gave in and agreed to ride one of his horses again. After all, it had been over a year since he dogged me to the press, so maybe things would be different this time.

Well, things sure were different, but in one of the worst ways imaginable.

Wayne put me on a well-bred horse named City Edition to ride in a race at Churchill Downs. When the gate sprang open, City Edition left running and I kept shouting "Whoa" to slow him down. As we were going around the turn, I heard a loud snap. Then all I could hear was the sound of hooves pounding around me as I flew face first onto the ground. Once I finished rolling from the impact, I lied there in the fetal position, trying my hardest not to get trampled. Meanwhile, I could see City Edition still trying to run, even though his right leg had snapped like a broken twig. He fell, but he got back up and he just kept running.

That was just the beginning of the nightmare. Calvin was right behind me when City Edition's leg shattered and his horse kicked me while Calvin tried to steer it away from the accident. Then as if in a movie, City Edition just kept on running until he battered into Robby's horse. Not knowing what hit him, Robby flew over his horse, sailing through the air and landing on the ground with a loud thud as his head smashed into the turf.

During that whole time, I couldn't think; I couldn't move. I was stuck to the ground in fear and I was helpless as I watched two of my best friends nearly get involved in a three-horse pileup. Calvin managed to get by uninjured, but Robby was lying on the ground and I honestly thought he was going to die that day.

As it turned out, Robby fractured his skull and I was lucky enough to get away with nothing but a bruised arm. City Edition wasn't quite as lucky, though. His leg broke so badly that the vets couldn't do anything for him. So the tarp went up, the ambulance stepped in, and a great horse was put to death.

Again, this was my first race with Wayne Lukas since he last put me in danger with another one of his crippled horses. And just to add insult to serious injury, Robby and I both made $50 that day for our sacrifices.

When I got out of the hospital, I went right over to see Robby in his hospital room. It killed me to see him in that condition and it killed even more to know the horse I was riding caused it. If I had just followed my gut and stayed away from Wayne and his crippled horses, chances are that none of this would have happened. But because of another not-so-freak accident on one of Wayne Lukas' horses, Robby had to have a metal plate put in his head and that was only because he was lucky enough not to die.

After that, the last thing I wanted to do was go back to Churchill Downs where everything had happened, but I had to ride the next day. So after one of the races, I took the route I always took and crossed Wayne's path like I always did. And wouldn't you know it, Wayne didn't have a single word to say to me. He didn't apologize. He didn't ask if I was okay. He didn't ask if Robby was even alive. He just kept on walking as if nothing had ever happened.

That day I made a vow that I would never ride for Wayne again. His silence spoke volumes and that day I saw his true colors. From then on, if I was going to race, it was going to be for a guy like Frankie Brothers, a man who cared about horses *and* jockeys.

Later that day, I grabbed my valet, the man who took care of all my gear, and said, "Get me something from Robby that I can bring with me." He got me one of Robby's shirts with his name on it. Feeling good about what I was about to do and what I would never do again, I put the shirt in my bag and left.

The next day, I was set to ride in the National Thoroughbred Training Association's All-Star Jockey Championship. As I set off for Texas, I stuck Robby's shirt in my bag and prayed to God that I would be able to put it to good use.

Being at that challenge was almost like being at the Kentucky Derby. There were thousands and thousands of people in the crowd and ESPN was there to record the whole event. Everybody beamed with excitement and anticipation as they waited to see who would be dubbed as the All-Star Jockey Champion.

I was accompanied by 11 other talented riders and we were going to ride in four races that ran by a point system. In each race, a jockey would get a horse that was rated from A to D, with A being the best quality. Each jockey would ride one horse from each category to make sure that the competition was fair. The races ran on a point system, so it didn't really matter where you placed. If you placed second in every race, that would be fine as long as someone else didn't place first in every race. Whoever wound up with the most points at the end of the four races would be the winner.

My competition was stiff and I knew that. But I also knew one other thing: I had to win this one for Robby. Camera crews were there to interview us jockeys before and in between the races. When the first newswoman came up to me, I couldn't contain my excitement. I lifted up my shirt and showed her Robby's shirt beneath it. I wanted the world to know that this night was for Robby. And when I showed his shirt on camera, I knew that whether I won or lost, Robby would still be able to know that this was all for him.

As the night went on, I raced on pure adrenaline in each of the four races. With my ambition egging me on, I rode the best I could. I rode like my life depended on it; like *Robby's* life depended on it. In the end, I won an unbelievable three out of four races, outpointing runner up Julie Krone by almost double.

When photographers started snapping pictures of me and the ESPN cameraman turned his camera my way, I lifted up my shirt for the world to see Robby's shirt beneath mine. I might have been the rider, but this day was all about Robby.

These races were for him and I wanted the world to know that. Robby was my brother, my protégé, and I wasn't going to let him lie in a hospital bed without knowing how much he was loved. I dedicated one of the proudest moments of my life to him because I knew that was the right thing to do.

That's the funny thing about love. It overpowers pride, anger, desire, and every other emotion. Whether you're talking about your love for your wife, your kids, or your dearest friends, love is still love.

And as that night proved – as my heart proved – my love for my friends and family was the strongest thing I would ever have.

Part 3

The Flip Side of Horse Racing

Chapter 15

Some people say that there's no such thing as perfection. You can train and practice and push yourself until you can't go any farther, but that will never make you perfect. It will make you good; it will make you better.

But perfect? There's no such thing.

I learned that lesson while I was at the pinnacle of my career and I thought that nothing could stop me. By that point, I had won two Breeders' Cup races and ridden horses that earned over $100 million in purses. I had ridden internationally in countries like Hong Kong, Japan, and Dubai, and I even received a beautiful gold Rolex watch as a gift from a Sheik. Just a little short of 4,000 wins, I was clearly great at what I did. I had ridden with the best, competed with the best, and oftentimes, won against the best. I knew that didn't make me perfect, but I knew I was as good as the rest.

Then one day in New Orleans, I was doing simple warm-ups on one of Frankie's horses. I was sitting there holding onto the reins, just jogging him and loosening him up before the race. He was a first time starter and I wanted him to get used to his new surroundings.

A horse jogged by us and my horse got spooked. He reared up on his hind legs, shying away from the other horse. The idea of jumping off crossed my mind, but I didn't get the chance. I just fell. I fell right off his back and landed on my feet.

At that time I didn't think. There wasn't time to weigh out my options. All I knew was that I couldn't let my spooked horse run around and spook the other horses, or worse, barrel into my fellow jockeys. So I grabbed back onto his reins – and I grabbed on the wrong way. Until that moment, I always held my horse from the right side. But on that day I fell the wrong way and I had to grab him from the left.

That was my first big mistake.

As I held on for dear life and tried to control him, I made a terrible judgment call and I knew it. I could control a horse while I was on top of it, but I certainly couldn't do it as I was being dragged along like a limp rag doll from the horse's side.

Well aware that I was doing the wrong thing, I held onto the horse for way too long. And that's when it happened.

The horse smashed its hind hoof down on the side of my knee and I knew right away that it was over. It felt like my knee was disconnected from the rest of my body, but I knew it was still there. The agony made that obvious.

But anything beyond that was yet to be known. Could I stand up? Could I walk away? I didn't know.

That's when I made my second big mistake and stood up.

The moment I stood up, I felt my knee buckle beneath me. This wasn't the kind of buckling you get after an amazing first kiss or after a slight trip over the carpet. This was the kind of sensation that only happens when your knee buckles in the literal sense.

When I looked down, I saw my knee physically split in two directions. Correction: I *felt* my knee separate in two directions. One half of my knee buckled to the left and the other half buckled to the right. What happened between the two halves remains a mystery.

I've seen a lot of things in my time, but I had never seen anything like that. I had never *felt* anything like that.

I expected to see blood, but surprisingly there wasn't any. All that existed was the cold, the mud, and a whole world of pain. And really, that's more than enough to ruin a man's day and maybe his life.

Time seemed to move in slow motion for me. I could see the people, my jockey friends racing towards me. I could feel my knee and the excruciating pain of my crushed kneecap. I could see the ambulance and the EMT van coming my way. I could see the horse acting like nothing had happened. I could see a lot of things, but none of them mattered.

All I could do was holler and scream.

My voice sounded shrill in my own ears and I just kept hollering and screaming. I screamed for my pain, for what had to be the end of my career, and for what would happen to my family now that I seemed to have two separate knees attached to one leg. I screamed at my own stupidity, at the concerned people who couldn't really understand what I was going through, and at the mud that made my murky situation all the worse.

Basically, I just screamed at everything. My career was over and I knew it. Nothing would ever be the same again.

I could hear random voices floating around me, but those voices sounded as disconnected from their owners as my knee felt disconnected from my body.

"Hang in there."

"Everything is going to be all right."

"You're going to be just fine."

"Modern medicine is going to get you back into shape in no time."

But even as I listened to everyone telling me how fine I would be, I knew it was all a lie. I didn't need to hear words. I could see the faces. And as I saw Frankie, my jockey friends, and the EMT's crowding around me in concern to tell me how fine everything would be, I could see the truth in their eyes.

My career really was over and I would never be the same again.

When I went to the hospital, it appeared that the doctors agreed with me. My knee had snapped, crackled, and popped like a bowl of fleshy Rice Krispies and they said I had a very low chance of recovering completely. I talked to a lot of doctors and all of them said the same thing. I would need a few surgeries and the chances of me ever riding again were slim.

I went through a reconstructive surgery in which the doctors tried to save what was left of my knee. They worked on my torn meniscus and the outside ligament. Then they cut out my MCL, one of the four major knee ligaments, because it was completely severed.

Now this is where the miracles of modern science I heard about stepped in.

The doctors took an MCL from a cadaver and replaced my torn ligament from bone to bone. Imagine that. My knee felt dead and now I had a dead part inserted in it to verify my feelings.

While I recovered, a lot of people tried to tell me the same things they told me at the time of my injury. Kelli, my family, and my friends all tried to cheer me up and show me the bright side of my situation. My knee wasn't completely ruined. I would be able to walk without crutches one day. Maybe I could even ride again if I tried hard enough.

But I knew those were nothing more than hopeful promises. Even as everyone tried to make me feel better, I could only keep repeating the words, "It's over. My career is over. My *life* that I've known since I was 11 is over."

And at that point, I really felt like everything was over. My surgery was successful, but it didn't perform miracles. When I recovered, I tried to ride again for about ten days, but it just didn't work; *I* just didn't work. I still had a lot of problems with my knee and if I ever wanted to ride like I used to, I knew I would have to have a second surgery.

So that's what I did.

Without anyone to accompany me on my journey, I boarded a plane to Williamsburg, West Virginia where one of the top athletic knee surgeons in the country could help me. Or at least I *hoped* he could help me.

When I got off the plane, I thought that West Virginia was one of the most gorgeous places I had ever seen. It was ice cold and my fingers were frozen from holding onto my crutches, but I could still see the beauty. I just wished I could have basked in the beauty with some of my loved ones by my side.

But alas, I was alone. Completely alone. Nobody came with me and nobody left there with me. All I had was myself, my crutches, and my hopes that the second surgery would work. So I went to the hospital and had an operation to clean up my knee, get rid of the scar tissue, and give me another chance to ride.

After that surgery, I was done. I was in a wheelchair and I couldn't stand. A machine had to keep my knee going while I slept so it wouldn't get stuck in place.

The problem was that *I* was stuck in place and in a bad one, at that. I couldn't stand, I couldn't ride, and I couldn't do anything else, either. All I could do was take my Vicodin every few hours and hope that the pain would eventually go away.

Well, the pain did eventually go away, but I'm sad to say that the Vicodin didn't. I couldn't function without my painkillers, especially since I had been on them for such a long time.

There were a few occasions when I tried to stop, but the withdrawals were brutal. One second I was cold and the next I was sweating. One minute I was crying and the next I was yelling. One day I was hungry and the next day I was vomiting. Everything about me was fucked up. So what did I do? I let myself get even more fucked up.

After a while, I found some doctors who recommended a 90-day stay in rehab. I didn't want to go to rehab, though. Rehab was a place for junkies and alcoholics. It wasn't a place for professional athletes; it wasn't a place for someone like me.

Or at least that's what I told myself.

Once I got there, I saw that I was wrong. Rehab doesn't discriminate based on social status, profession, or intelligence. Rehab is the one place where everybody is equal; where everybody is just as smart as everyone else because even though they once did something stupid, they're at least trying to get help.

And this may sound odd, but I was happy to see that rehab is for everyone. I was put in a rehab center full of doctors, lawyers, and other professionals. Even though I knew what it was like to live at the bottom, that didn't matter. Something about being with all of these professionals who were going through the same problems made me feel better about myself and what I was doing.

For 30 days, I lived in what felt like a posh prison or hospital wing. Every day was filled with personal counseling, group sessions, and drug tests. Like clockwork, these things happened at the same time every single day. Each day was the same as the next, but I didn't mind. That's what I needed.

So every day I sat in my room with two beds and one bathroom. I walked by the nurses' station and smiled at the nurses. I waved to the other people who stayed in the three or four rooms in the area. The layout of the place felt like a hospital wing, but that was okay. It passed as a really nice hospital.

One day I saw a tall, skinny guy walking around and he ended up becoming my roommate. I had already been in rehab for a while, but he was fairly new to the place. He was still coming off the drugs and I knew exactly what he was going through.

Soon we got to talking and he asked me what I did for a living. So I told him; or at least I told him what I *used to* do. Ironically, his family owned the oldest saddle making company in the country. They made the best Western saddles, like the ones John Wayne used on his horses. Given our ties to the horse world, we became really good friends really quickly.

But still, I felt like I needed to leave.

The doctors recommended that I stay for 90 days, but I couldn't do it. I wanted to see my family and try to pick up the pieces of what was left of my life. I was drug free and I thought that was good enough.

Did I stay clean on everything? Pretty much. I had a drink here or there, but that kept me from doing worse things.

Rehab showed me that I could still have fun – I could still be me – and I didn't have to resort to any pills or drugs to do so. Even though I probably should have stayed for the full 90 days, I wasn't ready to give up my emotions and the core of who I was. I didn't want to go that deep. I couldn't.

So I went home and I put my drug days behind me. When I got there, I found a really big box sitting out front of my house.

Inside was a beautiful black saddle that was nothing less than what John Wayne would expect for himself.

At that moment, I didn't know whether I would ever be able to put that saddle to good use. But I knew two things. I had made a great friend and I would do everything in my power to get back in the saddle again.

Chapter 16

Some people say that if you pray enough, God will automatically answer your cries. While I generally believe in that sentiment and I believe that God wants to help us, sometimes praying doesn't lead to miracles. You can pray and pray until you can't pray anymore and sometimes even that's not enough.

Sometimes you have to lend God a helping hand.

When I got out of rehab, I did everything I could to get myself back up on a horse. I visited doctor after doctor, hoping that one of them would eventually have good news for me. Unfortunately, they didn't. All of them said the same thing. My chances of riding again were next to impossible.

I fought with my regular doctor about it and tried to prove that I could get back in the game. He looked at me quite calmly and said, "Shane, you can't even bend down."

He asked me to get in a baseball catcher's position and I couldn't do it. My knee wouldn't bend back, no matter how hard I tried or prayed. I was still stuck in place and I couldn't possibly lie or beg or plead my way out of it.

My doctor saw me struggle and said, "How are you going to get back into racing? All your weight is on your knee and ankle, and your body can't handle the pressure. How are you going to get back on a horse?"

I knew that he was right but I didn't care. So I kept going to the doctor and when he couldn't help me, I started visiting my lawyers. I needed to know what to expect in the future and I was willing to take any professional opinion I could get.

The problem was that no one would tell me the words I wanted to hear. Nobody thought that I would ride again, but I didn't want to listen to any of them. I *couldn't* listen to any of them.

If I couldn't race, what would I do?

My only salvation was in knowing that I had a one million dollar insurance policy that I could cash out after two years. If I still couldn't ride after two years of rehabilitation, my accident policy had to pay out. My lawyers thought that was my best option. My wife thought that was my best option. My doctors thought that was my best option.

But I knew that I needed to ride again. I was a jockey, through and through, and nothing could stop me from living out my dreams.

So for over a year, I kept visiting the doctors, hoping that one day they would have better news for me. Sadly, they never did. Nobody believed that I would ever ride again, so I had to find a way to live like a 'normal' man.

I tried to do the kind of things a normal man does. I spent extra time with Kelli and our kids. I hung out with my jockey friends. I did everything that I used to do except for riding.

During that time, I did a lot of things, but one of my favorite activities was going to the karaoke bars. Mike Smith, Frankie Lovato, my fellow jockeys, and I always loved karaoke and we sang it as often as we could.

Even before I was injured, karaoke was a big part of our lives; of our brotherhood. We went to a karaoke party after every Kentucky Derby and one time I even got to sing with Ashley Judd.

Our karaoke days were great and we let them lead us right through my rehabilitation. One night my friend Randy Boudreaux wanted to go to a bar, so I brought him to a karaoke bar. I got up on the stage and sang my heart out, just like I always did. When my song ended, Randy said, "We need to get you to Nashville so you can record some songs."

Since Randy was so impressed by my voice, I figured that I should listen to him. After all, I had nothing to lose.

So I started working with Randy and we became great friends. Randy introduced me to a songwriter named Dennis Knudsen and suggested that I pay him to write songs for me. A few thousand dollars later I owned a bunch of songs, one of which was titled "Matthew, Mark, Luke and Earnhardt."

The tune to that song was really memorable and so were the words about the great NASCAR driver Dale Earnhardt. We knew that if we went about it the right way, we could make something of our song, so we got to work right away in the studio.

When I least expected it, one of my dreams came true. My musical icon Darryl Singletary heard my song and he thought that it had a catchy tune. Darryl, Randy, and I all went to a club to hang out and talk about music when the unthinkable happened.

Catastrophe struck.

During the last lap of the 2001 Daytona 500, Dale Earnhardt lost control of his car and crashed into a wall. At almost the same time as the winner of the race was driving into victory lane, the world was finding out that Earnhardt's injuries were more severe than anyone expected.

Within a few hours, NASCAR's President Mike Helton formally addressed the public and said, "Undoubtedly, this is one of the toughest announcements I've personally had to make. After the accident in Turn 4 at the end of the Daytona 500, we've lost Dale Earnhardt."

When we heard people talking about the announcement at the club, we couldn't believe what we were hearing. We all just looked at each other with the understanding that only a little while earlier on the way to the club, we had been listening to my song about Dale Earnhardt.

It was almost as if our song had been some kind of premonition; like we knew what was going to happen before the rest of the world had any idea.

Darryl, Randy, and I sat there shocked with a flurry of emotions overcoming us. Darryl didn't know what to think. Randy was thinking about the song. And all I could think was, "Oh my God. Dale Earnhardt is dead."

When we left the club that night, we listened to my song again. But this time we heard it with a whole different attitude and an entirely different meaning. Dale Earnhardt was really dead and we were listening to a song that could make his name live on in infamy even more than it was already bound to do on its own.

Randy had already let some people in Nashville listen to my demo CD, so the record companies knew that there was a song about Earnhardt the moment they heard about his death.

Shortly after, my phone was ringing off the hook and I had clusters of people who wanted to sign a contract with me. They wanted the song about Dale Earnhardt and they wanted it right away. In the end, DreamWorks won the publicity battle when they contacted me and gave me a record contract.

They were going to make me a country music star.

DreamWorks gave me a $25,000 advance for the record and taught me how to market it. They told me I would need to do a photo shoot, buy some new clothes, make a music video, and take on the persona of a star. So that's what I did.

Soon I had a music video on CMT and GAC, and my song jumped to number 56 on the Radio & Record charts. These accomplishments didn't come easily, but they did come. Randy and I traveled around the country in my Mercedes and pitched my record to everyone we could. I performed concerts at some of my favorite places, including a really special one at Gulfstream Park in Florida. As one of the racetracks that was always nice to me as a jockey, I was thrilled that they were just as kind when I switched careers. People welcomed my music with open arms and it looked like I may have found my new niche in life. I was well on my way to being a star and I was ready to receive all the benefits.

The problem was that there weren't any benefits.

Out of the $25,000 that I was promised, I ended up with a check for $7,500. Apparently I didn't see the fine print which stated that the photo shoot, music video, and new clothes that I needed were going to come out of my pay. I didn't know exactly what to expect in this unknown territory, but I didn't expect that all of the expenditures would come out of my pocket.

And after everything I had already been through with horse racing, I was sick of all the fine print in every industry. I didn't want to deal with it anymore.

I just wanted to be me. And the fact of the matter was that even though I loved country music, I was still a jockey at heart. So as quickly as it began, my music career ended. I walked away from the music world and tried to pick up where I left off in the horse racing industry.

My knee still wasn't perfect, but I still wanted to ride. I had to figure out whether I could ride again or if my career was really over. I had to make my decision quickly, though, because my time to cash out my insurance policy was running out. It had already been a year and a half since my injury and I only had six months left to figure out where my life would lead me next. If I was going to get back into horse racing, I had to do it soon.

I sat Kelli down and explained how important this was to me. I don't know where my confidence came from, but it was surely there. Since my injury, I had gained 32 pounds and even if I could get my knee back into shape, it would be torture to lower my weight that much. But still, I needed to do it. So I told my wife, "I know I can do it. I'm going to have to ride in pain, but I can do it."

Kelli was nervous and I could tell. She took my hand and said, "Baby, it's just too dangerous." She didn't want me to do it and she made that clear. Kelli agreed with the doctors and thought it was too risky. Plus, if I returned to riding before two years, I would lose my chance to cash out my policy.

I was adamant about what I wanted, though, and I wasn't willing to give up. Even though I could walk away with one million dollars if I retired, I just wasn't willing to do it. I wasn't *ready* to do it.

Soon I was given an offer that I didn't want to refuse. I could take $800,000 out of my insurance policy and give up the other $200,000 to go back and ride. That was a lot of money to give up, but I thought it was worth it.

So I sat Kelli down again.

This time I knew exactly what I wanted to tell her and the words just flew from my mouth. I was suddenly an orator and I had a verbal plan; a mission.

I said to her, "You know, this is my life. What they offered me is a lot of money and they gave me an opportunity to at least go back and try. I don't know if I can ride like I could, but I'm willing to try. Whatever happens, happens."

I could see the doubt in Kelli's eyes and I knew this was going to take more convincing. I pleaded, "Just let me go back. I'll make back the money I'm giving up. I promise. I'll get my remaining 248 wins and go out with a total of 4,000 wins. And this time we'll have money put away so I won't have to ride everyday. I won't have to ride 5,000 claimers just to ride good horses. I won't have to take the bullshit or play the politics. I can ride what I want. I can be *me* now."

The more I spoke, the more excited I got. I could really go out there and be me. I wouldn't have to play by the political rules anymore or pretend to be someone I wasn't. I could get back in the jock's room and continue listening to everyone's opinions. And since I wouldn't be involved in the politics anymore, I could get out there and make some real differences.

All of the problems that jockeys faced regarding weight issues, low pay, and low insurance policies could change. I could make sure of it. Since most of the other jockeys had the same opinions as me, we could surely make some changes for the better. We were a band of brothers and we could do anything we put our minds to.

I was pumped and Kelli knew it. The more she listened to me, the more she seemed to agree with what I had to say; the more I could see she trusted me. Things would really be different now. I could have it all: my family, my friends, my career, and my life. And this time it would all be different; it would be better.

Before long, Kelli said, "Yes," and I got ready to ride again. Injured knee or not, my racing career was beginning anew. And this time when I went back, I was determined to bring the horse racing industry to its knees.

Chapter 17

A lot of people share the common misconception that jockeys are naturally light. We just popped out of our mamas being light, agile, and strong enough to control a horse. Our physical conditions are natural and we were made this way.

Well, I'm here to tell you that everyone who thinks that is wrong.

There are some riders who are naturally light enough to meet the absurdly low jockey weight limits. For instance, Pat Day probably doesn't weigh more than 100 pounds because that's the way he was built. But for the rest of us who aren't Pat Day, we have to work to keep our weights down.

What does that mean exactly? It means a bunch of things and none of those things are very pretty.

I'm not going to name names and I'm not going to speak on behalf of every jockey who has an eating disorder. But I am going to tell you a bit about what I went through to keep *my* weight down throughout my riding career and what I saw 90 percent of riders do to some extreme.

To start with, I barely ate. I woke up every morning, popped a diet pill, drank a bit of coffee, and then headed over to the track. I worked horses, worked myself, and worked up an appetite in the process. When I got hungry, I didn't eat. I couldn't. If I wanted to ride, I had to keep my weight around 112 pounds. And since I rode every day, I couldn't let my weight slip.

Even if I had a few days or even a week off between races, it wouldn't have mattered. Jockeys are weighed before and after every race. There's a scale in the jocks' room where a track official called a Clerk of Scales makes sure we "weigh out" at the correct weight before the race. Then there's another scale right next to the winner's circle. Right after a win, jockeys weigh in again to make sure they carried the weight they were supposed to carry.

Though some people could lie about their weights – a point we'll get to later – we generally needed to keep our weights as low as we could. If we got caught over the weight limit, we were immediately disqualified.

Since it only took a split moment of weakness for a jockey to put back on all the weight he worked to keep off, it was best not to indulge and to just stick by the unspoken rules of horse racing.

I would sit in the jocks' room talking with the other jockeys, but sometimes I wasn't really listening. All I could focus on was the smell of the hamburgers, hot dogs, french fries, and other foods that wafted into the room from the jocks' kitchen. I never understood why an establishment that was so strict on weights would tempt us with such fattening foods, but there was really no point wondering. The jocks' room is what it is, and the fattening food is the least of the problems that go on in there.

So I tried to ignore the smell of greasy heaven and to carry on with my day, but there always came a point when I had to eat. So when that point hit, that's what I did. I ate.

And then I promptly threw it back up into the heaving bowl.

When I talk about the heaving bowl, I'm not talking about a standard toilet, either. In the racing world, it's common knowledge that jockeys have to resort to extreme measures to keep their weights down. The heaving bowls are just one of the ways that we are allowed – or maybe even encouraged – to do that.

Since the industry needs us to make racing possible, they try to accommodate our low weight crusades in any way they can. They provide us with all sorts of fattening foods for when we get hungry and most jocks' rooms have at least one special commode that's referred to as a heaving bowl.

Calling it a bowl is a bit inaccurate because it's more like a square. It looks like a toilet as far as porcelain and handles go, but that's where the similarities end. A heaving bowl is enormous and it has one main purpose: for jockeys to flip their food without clogging the pipes. Apparently there have been problems with toilets clogging over flipping sessions, so a lot of jocks' rooms installed special commodes to make heaving easier.

To add insult to injury, some facilities charge a fine to anybody who is caught heaving in a standard toilet. There are actually signs posted that state the fines for heaving in a non-heaving bowl.

That's the 'flip side' of horse racing that nobody wants the public to know about.

Before I got hurt, I didn't think very much about what we did to keep our weights down. I didn't pay attention to the fact that most of us had eating disorders and that we were literally sweating to death in the hot box. I didn't like what we went through, but those behaviors were all considered natural in the jockey world.

But once I finally got out of the game, I saw that there was nothing natural about it.

While I prepared myself to ride again, I had to drop 32 pounds to meet the weight limits and I had to drop it fast.

One day I took a break from all of my training and dieting and I went out for drinks with Kenny Desarmeux and Randy Romero. We were sitting around and a documentary reporter named Kate Davis started talking to us. She was interested in doing a story on Randy and we were answering all her questions. Then, out of nowhere, Kenny chimed in and said, "If you want to do a story, maybe you should do a real story. Do a story on the depression and the sickness and the passing out ... Just do a real story."

Randy and I looked at each other in shock. We looked at Kenny with even more shock. Then we turned our heads back to the reporter, feeling more shocked than ever. Just when we thought we reached our shock limit, Kenny continued, "Why don't you tell them about the flipping bowls and about the hidden black secrets that nobody wants to talk about?"

Needless to say, Randy and I reached a point beyond shock when Kenny brought that up and Kate's mouth was opened as wide as ours were.

We sat there in silence for a while, all of us lost in our own thoughts. Randy was surprised by the change in scope of the

156

original documentary. I was thinking about how beneficial it might be to educate the public on what really goes on behind closed jocks' doors. Kenny was pleased as punch that he had the courage to set the wheels of change in motion. And I'm sure that Kate was thinking something like, "Oh my God, this is going to win me an Emmy."

When the silence finally ended, we all realized we had a real story on our hands. One thing led to another, and before I knew it, the scope of the documentary had changed. This documentary wasn't just going to be about Randy anymore. It was going to be about the underbelly of horse racing that most people are not willing to talk about.

And since one of my main reasons to get back into the game was to improve the sport, I had no problem talking to my heart's content.

When Kate asked me about jockey weights, I wasn't afraid to answer her honestly. Since the system was good enough for the racetracks to put us through it, then it must have been good enough for the public to know about it.

So I told her everything. I talked about the countless hours of sweating in the hot box, the special heaving bowls in most jocks' rooms, and the diuretics, laxatives, appetite suppressants, and other pills that most jockeys took to keep their weights down.

Then I took things one step further and explained that this wasn't a personal choice; it was an unspoken racing requirement.

The racing authorities never specifically told us what to do to make weight; they condoned what we were doing. Some jocks' rooms were lined with toilets that had 'No Heaving' signs behind them while they contained a bigger commode especially made for heaving. Every jocks' room had a hot box with no maximum time requirements.

These things were there for a reason.

As I explained all of this to Kate and gave her a personal tour of the Churchill Downs jocks' room, I asked her, "Do you think they know what we're doing in here? Yeah, they know. But do they care that we're in here killing ourselves? No, they don't. They're willing to give us whatever they can to help us make weight. Whatever we need, they give it."

That is, they were willing to give us anything that would lower our weights, but not to improve the quality of our health.

Now here we are, a bunch of professional athletes who put our lives on the line to ride, and we're being killed from the inside out. You wouldn't see something like that happen to a football or baseball player or any other kind of athlete. If that happened, it would be all over the news. When it comes to jockeys, the world doesn't know what we go through, so these problems must not exist.

But these problems do exist and as the HBO documentary *Jockey* showed, all of us have to go through the problems in our own way. I had to extremely reduce my weight to get back into riding after my injury. Randy needed to have a kidney transplant because of all his years of reducing. And new jockey Chris Rosier was just beginning to see what life was like for a blooming jockey.

All of us had problems and hardships, but at that point, things were certainly hardest on Randy. I'll never forget sitting in his hospital room with him, crying over what happened to one of my dearest friends. He needed a new kidney, but that's something that he would never get if it was up to the jockey insurance benefits – or lack thereof.

As a jockey, you don't get health insurance for you and your family, dental insurance, or even a retirement plan. It's up to you to save your money – if you're one of the lucky few who makes enough money – for a rainy day. So for a jockey like Randy who needed a new kidney and certainly wouldn't be able to ride again, financial help from the industry was never going to come.

That's why some of the other jockeys and I took matters into our own hands. We put on a fundraiser for Randy, trying our hardest to buy him the kidney he needed, or at least to give him enough money to survive until he could find money another way. The fundraiser was like a big party, filled with jockeys, trainers, horse owners, and Randy's personal friends and diehard fans. I even got to play with a fantastic band straight out of Nashville to keep the atmosphere light and make sure everyone had a good time.

Simultaneously thrilled and overwhelmed by the crowd, I was excited to see my good friend Frankie Lovato standing amidst the people. When I saw him, a huge smile broke across my face. I grabbed onto Frankie's sleeve and said, "Frankie! Come here! There are some people I want you to meet." I pulled him through the crowd and led him to the backdoor where we could easily get to the tour bus. Shouting over the music and the crowd, I said, "Come on; I want you to meet the band."

Frankie and I stepped into the tour bus and I introduced him by saying, "This is my good friend Frankie Lovato. This is one guitar playing SOB. Can he do a song with the band tonight?" The band, of course, agreed to let Frankie play with us and I was completely pumped. Playing with Frankie brought back terrific memories of days when we used to sit together and sing for fun. And just like in those old days, as we got closer to the stage, I leaned into Frankie's ear and said, "What if I forget the words?" Frankie laughed at me like he always did when I said that and he reassured me that I wouldn't forget anything. As usual, Frankie was right. I remembered the words to every song and the concert was a hit. Even more importantly, the fundraiser was a hit and we raised more money for Randy than we could have ever expected.

That was one of the most special events of my life and I still grin from ear to ear whenever I see parts of it captured on Kate Davis' documentary. Not only did I have a fantastic time that night, but I felt blessed that Randy might be able to actually get that kidney that he desperately needed. And since his struggle was captured on film, maybe – just maybe – the public would step in and help with our cause, too.

Once *Jockey* aired, people were as shocked as I expected them to be. Robert Clay, the owner of the famous Kentucky thoroughbred horse farm Three Chimneys, wrote me a letter praising me and thanking me for standing up for jockey weights. Even the legendary musical genius Burt Bacharach, who is also a prominent horse owner in California, was so outraged by what jockeys go through that he posted a full page advertisement in the *Daily Racing Form* to promote jockey weight awareness before Belmont Day.

A lot of other influential people got involved in the previously secret world of jockey eating disorders after the documentary, too. For instance, I was invited to appear on a one hour CNN special with Paula Zahn called "Walking the Thin Line." This special featured Jane Fonda, Jamie-Lynn DiScala from *The Sopranos*, and a couple of other people who struggled with eating disorders.

The interview was surreal and Paula really gave me a new perspective on my lifestyle. Although she was speaking to the audience, she opened my eyes to things I never saw before. She explained my situation to her viewers and said, "When not on the racetrack, he also ran for hours in layers of heavy sweat suits. When he finished, he would have his wife, Kelli, wrap him up in blankets to make sure he lost even more weight."

That was like a slap that brought me back to reality. Kelli used to do that for me all the time, but I never really thought about it. That was just something that I thought I had to do. I still think about the way that Kelli responded to Paula and it drives me mad to think that I wasn't just doing this to myself; I was doing it to my family.

Kelli told Paula, "I was in fear of him having a heart attack. I would try to peel the clothing off of him. And he's like, wait, no, leave it a little longer. I would cry, like, what do you mean?" She described how she wanted to cool me off and help, and how she just cried all the while.

While Kelli relived this common occurrence on screen, I felt like crying because I could physically feel her words when she revealed, "I felt like, in a way, I was almost helping him to – to – to kill himself."

That moment was horrible for me and all I wanted to do was pull Kelli into my arms and tell her that she would never have to worry about things like that again. The problem was that I still wanted to ride, so I knew deep down that we would probably have to go through the same exact things again.

Even as I sat there talking to Paula Zahn and telling her that I could eat like a normal man now, I knew that my battle with eating disorders wouldn't be over. But at least I had the realization that what I was doing was wrong.

During all this time, my doctor was furious with me for what I was doing to myself. I was only riding at two or three percent body fat and he said anything under five percent is extremely dangerous. My doctor told me what I was doing to myself and to my organs. He told me that I couldn't survive this way. My organs were cannibalizing themselves and I could not last this way for much longer.

The idea of my organs eating themselves scared me; it terrified me. I wanted to stop putting my body through this torment but I didn't know how.

I had been through hell since the time of my knee injury and all I wanted to do was ride again. I missed the feeling of being on a horse and riding towards victory. I missed the pride and the glory and the happiness that racing brought to my life. Even though I hated what I had to go through to achieve those feelings, I still missed racing.

I wanted the industry to improve and make weights higher, but I knew that wouldn't happen in a day. So if I wanted to get back into the game and make some changes, I still had 32 pounds to lose.

And when your natural body weight is somewhere around 150 pounds, it's impossible to drop down to 112 pounds in a healthy way.

So what did I do? I continued to heave and sweat and starve and take diet pills. I kept doing all of the things that I had done before, but this time there was one difference:

I wanted the torture to stop.

I knew it was going to take some time and that I would need some help from my fellow jockeys, but I was confident that we could make some serious changes. After all, if you don't have jockeys, you can't have horse racing. It's as simple as that. As long as we could band together like the brothers that we were, there was no way for us to fail.

And since the industry certainly wouldn't want the sport to stop, they would have to succumb to our needs.

Or at least that's what I thought.

Chapter 18

Here's a little known fact for you: the first six riders to win the Kentucky Derby were former slaves who had been forced to start riding before slavery was abolished.

You may think that's coincidental; that former slaves were popular in the Kentucky Derby because Kentucky just had a lot of slaves back then. If you ask me, former slaves were the first Derby riders because nobody else in their right mind would want to compete in such a dangerous sport.

Now here is where the past meets the present. Times have changed, but the rules of the Kentucky Derby have not changed in over 90 years. In the first Kentucky Derby, all jockeys rode at 100 pounds. The required impost rose over the years, until in 1920 the Derby riding weight was set at 126 pounds – like it was set in stone.

When the Derby began in 1875, people were naturally smaller; most of them were starving. In a time when food was not readily available and vitamins were not added to most foods, it was considered normal for people to weigh 126 pounds or under. In fact, it was normal for people to weigh 112 pounds or under like the lowest riding weights most modern races still require.

Nowadays things have changed. We have an abundance of food and people are naturally much larger. That's partly why obesity has become such a big problem. There's more than enough food to go around and people are evolving; they're expanding.

So in a time when we have the means to eat and we no longer have to worry about when our next meal will come, it's more than a little barbaric that professional athletes have to starve if they want to maintain their careers.

Other countries have caught on to that idea and they've adjusted their weight limits accordingly. In Australia, hot boxes are illegal because a jockey died in one. In New Zealand, jockeys must weigh in at a minimum of 127 pounds. In Chile, jockeys are allowed to ride at weights as high as 132 pounds. In the Middle East, jockeys can compete in any race so long as they weigh 126 pounds or less.

But here in the United States, the Land of the Free, jockeys have to keep their weights around 112 pounds for standard races. Otherwise, they'll be have no place in the game.

Basically, we're still being treated like slaves today.

The exception to this American weight rule is in the Kentucky Derby, our country's greatest racing event. In other races, these horses are used to running one and an eighth miles with about 112 pounds on their backs. But in the Derby, they have to run further than they've ever run before, going one and a quarter miles with up to 126 pounds on their backs.

So if a horse can physically handle a 14 pound weight increase on a longer run, why in the world can't we raise the weight limit for standard races by a few pounds?

That was the stand I took when I publicly spoke about low jockey weights and I was greeted by many unhappy faces after the specials aired. Some people in the industry couldn't believe that I had the gall to reveal the truth on national television. They felt that it was wrong to speak out against an industry that I loved and worked in, even though I spoke to improve the industry and all who are involved in it.

The main person who publicly disagreed with my plight was Wayne Lukas; the arch nemesis of jockey health, if you will.

While Randy Romero was lying in the hospital, fighting for his life, *USA Today* printed an article about him and jockey weight limits. The article described all that Randy went through to maintain his low weights and nobody with a heart could feel less than repulsed by what they read.

Randy's kidney specialist Dr. Duff said that Randy had renal failure because of a combination of his burns from the hot box, his flipping, and his constant dehydration. To make matters worse, Randy was infected with Hepatitis C which he believes he got during a blood transfusion after he was scorched in the hot box. Even if he could get a kidney transplant, it wouldn't do any good. His Hepatitis would reject the new kidney and then he would be right back where he started. So the documentary, the fundraiser, and everything else that was done for Randy was done in vain. He could not get a new kidney now or ever. One of my closest friends was doomed to die.

And Randy probably would not have suffered through any of these problems if it was not for the outdated jockey weight limits.

During that time, the Jockey's Guild was trying to make some serious changes in jockey weights. We started looking into body fat percentages and the repercussions of having too little body fat. Even Pat Day fought for this cause, despite the fact that he didn't think that a weight increase would be a permanent solution to the problem.

The Guild got together as an organization and we riders decided that we were going to grandfather in the riders who were already licensed. Then we would raise the weights and any new rider who had less than five percent body fat would not be allowed to compete.

In other words, we were about to abolish the torture that so many young jockeys faced.

But still, Wayne Lukas stood his ground and testified that there was no need for us to try to increase the weight limits. He believed that the weights were fine and that they should remain the same for the sake of the sport. As he stated in the *USA Today* article, "I am concerned that if we increased the weight we could have more breakdowns. Most people agree that speed and weight are detrimental to a horse's longevity."

Is that so, Mr. Lukas?

I would say that a jockey who is so sick that he can barely see straight is detrimental to a horse. I might say that the rising number of jockey deaths that stem from eating disorders is detrimental to the image of horse racing. I could even go so far as to say that the amount of skilled jockeys who will eventually leave the sport to favor their health over money could be detrimental to a horse's racing career.

But adding five pounds to a weight limit that was established over 100 years ago? That won't make a lick of a difference to a horse.

Unfortunately, everybody puts Wayne on such a pedestal that his words might as well be the Gospel. They don't realize that Wayne's horses rarely make it beyond two or three years. They don't realize that he willingly puts injured horses out on the track and jeopardizes their lives as well as the lives of the jockeys. They most certainly don't realize that Wayne went so far as to make one of his jockeys lie to the vet about the state of his horse. So to the millions of people who read that *USA Today* article, Wayne was right and the jockey weights should remain the same.

And maybe Wayne was right. Maybe *his* horses couldn't handle extra weight because of the state of soundness they were in to begin with. But other horses, horses that were given the care they needed, could easily handle extra weight without giving them any extra mental or physical strain.

In a sad attempt to show his supposed compassion for jockeys, Lukas ended his segment of the article by stating, "I would say if a jockey is jeopardizing his health, he should seek other employment."

What an interesting world that would be. In my estimation, more than half of American jockeys battle life threatening eating disorders and push themselves beyond their personal boundaries to lose weight. Almost every jockey utilizes the hot box, even if they only go in to shave like Pat Day does. Almost every jockey has heaved or resorted to diet pills at least a couple of times so that they can make weight for a race. Almost every jockey has done things that other professional athletes would never consider doing because that is just part of the sport.

So what would be left if all of those jockeys sought other employment like Wayne Lukas suggested?

Nothing, that's what.

If you ask me, the truth of the matter is that Wayne Lukas did not fight against an increase in weight limits to protect horses, nor did he fight against higher weight limits to make the game fair for jockeys. He fought against all that because his soul is buried in the darkest recesses of the industry.

Wayne knows what goes on in the horse racing world, but he doesn't want anybody to know. As one of the best politicians in the game, he follows the hush-hush example of the higher powers in the industry and he keeps his mouth shut about every issue that could potentially make the industry better and stronger.

And that's the real problem with Wayne and the industry, itself. Nobody is willing to open their mouth and expose the truth. No one wants to talk about the calamities that jockeys have suffered. Nobody wants to talk about the fact that when the crowd sees a green curtain go up during a race, there is a euthanized horse on the other side of that curtain being hauled away into a horse ambulance by a chain around its neck. No one wants to talk about any of these things because they know they would get the kind of disapproving looks I got after I spoke out about jockey weight disorders.

But the fact of the matter is that bad things do happen to jockeys and the world has no idea. The darker side of horse racing is covered up so that nobody will be the wiser.

Have you ever heard anyone mention the two young men who died from being in the hot box?

I highly doubt it.

But just because the public didn't know about it doesn't mean that it didn't happen. About two years ago, a young jockey named Chris Herell broke his shoulder. While he recovered, he gained a lot of weight and pulled 26 pounds in the hot box within one month so he could get back into the game. Then one day he just collapsed and died.

In another instance, a young Puerto Rican boy named Emanuel Jose Sanchez pulled seven pounds, rode in his race, and prepared to go home. When he finished his race, he was given the option to ride in a new opening in the last race of the day. He agreed to ride in that second race, so he took his street clothes off, got back in the hot box, and pulled some more weight. He turned the shower on and the second the cold water hit him, he was done. He gave his life for the chance to ride one more race.

You didn't hear about this in the racing magazines, on the news, or anywhere else. But I'm telling you about this now. I want you to remember the names Chris Herrell and Emanuel Jose Sanchez because they died for no reason.

They died because people like some people are so deep in the politics of the industry that they made sure nobody would ever know what could happen or what did happen.

If Wayne hadn't come out and spoken against a weight increase in *USA Today*, the Jockey's Guild could have very likely made the changes that we needed. Chris Herrell and Emanuel Jose Sanchez may not have been able to ride, but the point is that they would still be alive.

But in one brief moment and one harsh statement, Wayne Lukas ruined the chances of that happening.

So when Wayne Lukas has the gall to come out and say that we can't raise the weights because that would be detrimental to the horse, I just have one thing to say. Wayne is the one who is detrimental to the horse *and* the jockey.

The fact that he could sit there and watch the color drain from Randy Romero's face and to witness one of the world's greatest jockeys dying a slow death without a pang of guilt says something. It screams something.

So really, I can't be all that surprised that he publicly slammed me after I spoke out about weights and that he hindered all of the progress that the Jockey's Guild was trying to make. I think that's just in his character.

But the moment Wayne decided to declare war against me, I was ready to take him on. It was time to band together with the rest of the jockeys who were as concerned as I was. It was time for us to show the horse racing industry that it would be nothing without us.

There will never be a day when ten monsters can come barreling out of a starting gate with nobody on their backs. And since I knew that my jockey friends had my back, I wasn't going to hold up the white flag any time soon.

Chapter 19

Most sports are taken care of by governing bodies that protect and fight for their athletes. When people in the NFL, NBA, PGA, or any other major sports group need something, there are more than enough people who will fight for them. But if you're a jockey who wants to see changes in the industry, you have to fight for yourself.

When I started riding again, I remember being in the hot box, pulling weight with some other jockeys. We were talking about the weights and about what we could do to change them; to fight for our health. There were a lot of different ways that we could try to make a difference, but the most logical one was to just be honest. If we wanted to increase the weights, we were going to have to stop kidding ourselves and the industry.

I've already explained what a lot of jockeys go through to maintain their low weights, but there's one thing that I've neglected to mention. Even with all of the eating disorders, diet pills, and hot box sessions, we *still* couldn't make weight. For most of us, there was just no way to get our weights down to the 112 pounds we needed to ride in a race.

So what did we do? We lied.

It may not be right, but it was our only option. We could either confess that we were riding six or seven pounds overweight and get taken off our mounts or we could lie. With families to feed and careers to nourish, our choices were really quite limited.

But on that particular day as I sat in the hot box, I had an idea. Instead of marking down that we all weighed 112 pounds, we should write something a bit closer to the truth. We should all write that we weighed 116 pounds because that's what I wanted the low weight point to be. I didn't think it was necessary to aim for 126 like the Kentucky Derby limit, but I thought that a high point of 122 was reasonable.

We knew that none of us were riding at 116, let alone 112, so that was a great place to begin. If we all wrote down weights higher than the ones we were assigned, there was no way that we could all get taken off our horses. How could anybody fight against that? The races had to go on and they couldn't do that without jockeys. Just by marking down a four pound difference, we could potentially make all the difference in the world.

So when I got out of the hot box, I marked my weight down as 116. I didn't look at the scale. I doubted that I was even near 116, but that didn't matter. I had pulled as much weight as I could and that was the best I could do. Now I was making a stand and I expected my friends to follow suit.

Unfortunately, things didn't go the way I planned. The other jockeys got out of the hot box and marked their weights at 112, just like they always did.

At the time, I felt like I had been stabbed in the back. I went out there and put my neck on the block for my fellow riders, but nobody followed. I paved the way for them to make some real changes; for them to better themselves and the industry. Still, they didn't have the courage to follow.

I looked at my fellow jockeys and asked them, "Where do you draw the line?" I argued and I fought, but it didn't accomplish anything. The rest of the jockeys weren't ready to put their careers on the line for the hope of a better career and lifestyle.

I hoped that maybe the Jockey's Guild would take a stand and support me, but that didn't happen, either. Everything carried on as it always had before, but this time I felt like I was being shunned just as much as I was back in Erath. Some people supported my fight, but most wanted to keep their hush-hush attitudes and pretend that nothing ever happened.

On the other hand, some people were appalled by the situation and wanted things to change. For instance, my buddy Ken Patin, who became my valet when I recovered from my injury, supported my every move. He knew what it was like to try and make weight and he knew how many people lied about what the scales read. As both a jockey and a valet, he supported my fight for higher weights because he knew the truth about everything.

But most people thought that I was just trying to cause a ruckus; that jockey weights were not nearly as detrimental as I portrayed them to be; that maybe those two boys spontaneously died for no reason. They thought that all riders were just little; that we were all just like Pat Day. But Pat Day and the other smaller riders were the minority, the exception, the throw-back to the old days. They weren't the norm anymore and I knew it. I rode all over the world with the best of the best, all cheating the scales.

None of us were honest before and nobody wanted us to be honest now.

The problem was that every lie came with a price. All of the top jockeys could get into nearly any jocks' room at any track and get away with just about anything. The underdogs, though, they couldn't get away with a single thing.

When I was at my peak, getting ready to ride in a half million or a million dollar race, I would go into a jocks' room without even thinking about my real weight. I would get in the hot box, pull the most I could, and then get on the scale without even looking. It didn't matter if I really weighed 112 pounds. I hardly ate, I flipped whatever I did eat, I took diet pills and diuretics, I spent hours in the hot box, and I did everything I could do to be as light as I could be. So the real number on the scale didn't mean anything. I did the best I could do and people were willing to accept that because I won so many races.

As was the case with the other top riders, there wasn't a place in the country where I really needed to make weight. If I flew into some city to ride and a trainer was concerned about my extra pounds, people would say, "Oh, he's good. Don't worry about it." The other leading riders and I would get our clearance and get ready to ride, no matter what our real weights were.

Some clerks weren't nearly as lenient, though, and it took a bit of persuasion for them to let us get by on the scales. We would slip some money into their hands, get on the scale, and then prepare for our mounts. Most of the time we didn't even look at the scale because we knew we really didn't have to.

But then I would see those kids who were barely making a living from racing; less fortunate kids riding bummed horses. I watched those kids riding horses maybe five times a week and getting paid about $50 a ride for their sacrifices. They heaved and sweated and did everything they could to conform to the industry. That didn't matter, though. If they were even a half-pound overweight, the trainer would switch riders.

Meanwhile, the prima donnas of the sport could get away with being five, six, or seven pounds over without any consequences. We could get away with anything because of who we were. We were the superstars of the industry – the riding aces the betting public and fans of the sport came out to see.

It just wasn't right. As a human being, I knew it was all wrong. I was in Hell and I had the industry on my side. Those poor kids were standing next to me in Hell for $50 and they couldn't get away with a half pound. And those were the kids who were whipping their own asses to make a living. They were earning their money, riding in as many races as they could for $50 a mount. Just as the sport needs its stars, it also needs the ordinary guys who ride the ordinary horses. They help the industry flourish and they're the ones who have to pay for it.

The whole situation made me sick.

I felt like garbage and I couldn't even imagine what those kids felt like. I was suffering, watching everyone else suffering, and riding all over the country knowing that none of the big dogs were doing their weights. It was plain wrong.

The Jockey's Guild should have helped us, but somewhere along the line, they sold their souls to the industry. The Guild wasn't always that way, though. In the beginning, the group was formed because a lot of jockeys weren't getting paid for their work. A group of men banded together to fight for what was right and they changed the industry because of it.

Keeping those original Guild members in mind, I knew that I would have to do the same thing. I had to fight for myself, for the kids who stood behind me, and for the guys who stood before me.

Something needed to be done about the current problems, but it's hard for an army of one to take on the entire industry. Nobody wanted to follow and there was only so much that I could do by myself.

So I kept my head up high and kept riding. I was doing great again, but I was not at my highest potential. My weight was not good. I had to take diet pills every morning to get through the day. My weight had never been past 126 pounds, but I went up to 140 pounds after the injury. It was hard to get my weight down because I was older; my body was bigger than it had ever been before. I was aggravated at myself because I knew I didn't look the same on a horse and I was even more aggravated that I would have to look sickly again to look the same.

After a while, the weight issue really started to circulate around the industry again. Major magazines and newspapers published articles about weights. Jockeys started talking with doctors and nutritionists. And I kept on fighting just the same as I had since the time of my injury.

The weight issue hit its peak in 2004 when the infamous 'overweight jockey scandal' began. Two clerks of scales from New York named Braulio Baeza and Mario Sclafani were charged with letting jockeys cheat the scales. They were in some serious trouble and they had to go up against a grand jury to determine their fates.

When the State offered me immunity to testify in front of the grand jury, I didn't really know what they expected of me. So I said, "Okay, offer me immunity and I'll go." At the time, I didn't understand what was really going on. Braulio Baeza had been one of the best jockeys ever. He was a Hall of Famer; one of my idols. He put his job on the line, he rode, he did interviews. But why was he being prosecuted?

Furthermore, why were my friends Mark Guidry, Robby Albarado, and three other jockeys in trouble? Were they really going to go to jail because someone said that they were cheating the scales?

Unclear of what was about to happen, I went to the trial to support the clerks and the jockeys. I didn't know what to expect when I got there. I almost expected to see a group of stern men in powder white wigs wagging their fingers at everyone involved.

When I got there, though, I saw that everything I expected was completely wrong.

I walked into the room and there were just a bunch of people sitting there; normal people in regular clothes, looking like they were on a field trip to the movie theatre. The State's attorney came up to me and told me that it was time to testify in front of the regular audience. When I approached the witness seat, I wasn't nervous. I just sat there and answered all of the questions that came my way.

The attorney asked me, "Did you ever see those men lying about their weights?"

I looked him in the eye and said, "No."

He looked right back at me and replied, "Oh really? Well, what about this day when your horse was supposed to carry 116 pounds and you weighed out at 126?"

I responded, "I don't know. Maybe the scale messed up. It's not my fault."

Then I took things one step further and made sure that the attorney knew exactly what he was dealing with. I said, "But you want to know how it is? I haven't eaten all day long. I get up in the morning to work horses and I don't eat breakfast. I might drink a cup of coffee and then I start pulling weight."

I continued, "When I walk in there, I jump on the scales to see where I'm at and then I go back in the box and I sweat. I pull as much weight as I can. Then when I can't pull any more, I go and take my shower. I walk over to the scales, go to my room – my little corner – and put my silks on. I don't look at the scales. I report 116 because I've been reporting 116 for ten years. They call number six, I grab my stuff and get on the scale, but I don't look when anybody else goes on the scale. It's none of my business."

Still looking directly at the attorney, I concluded with, "So what the scale says, I don't know. But I do know that I did everything in my power to lose weight and that I'm riding at two percent body fat. I can't take any more off."

Apparently that was all the State needed to hear from me. I didn't want to get anybody in trouble. I didn't want anybody to lose their jobs. I just wanted people to know what we jockeys went through every day.

In a way, I'm sure my point was heard. Unfortunately, the prosecution also made its point and the clerks both lost their jobs forever. That wasn't what I was aiming for in my speech and I still feel terrible that those two men lost their careers.

Did anything good come about from that trial? Not really. The only good thing was that people were finally seeing jockey weight limits for what they were. And when it comes to any type of revolution, awareness is always the first step.

Chapter 20

If you take a look through history, you'll see that change never comes easily. Americans didn't want to pay taxes on tea, so dumped their problem in Boston Harbor. King Henry VIII wanted a divorce, so he started a new religion. Metallica didn't want anyone stealing their songs, so they prosecuted people from Napster. And I wanted jockeys to ride without heaving, so I gave up a potential Hall of Fame career.

Before I deeply involved myself in the fight for weights, things were going wonderfully for me. I won thousands of races, made millions of dollars, and earned the respect of fans around the world.

I started using my money for good, trying to help other people who were not as financially fortunate as I was. I started up a scholarship fund at the high school in Erath and helped some of the kids from my hometown get into college. The first year, nobody contacted the recipient of the scholarship, so it was awarded to somebody else when he didn't show up at the ceremony. I felt so bad for that kid that I gave him a scholarship, too. From that point on, I chose two winners every year – one boy and one girl – so that at least a couple of kids from Erath would have a fair shake at life.

Around that time, Joe Deaver contacted me to see if I wanted to get involved with the Gary Gupton Golf Tournament. Both Joe and Gary had children with Down's Syndrome, and they used that tournament to raise money for research, new schools, familial help, and other forms of financial assistance. The tournaments did very well every year, but they got even better once I got involved. The Gary Gupton and Shane Sellers Golf Tournaments raised a ton of money. Last year it was so successful that the Shriners gave $1.5 million towards the cause. Everybody who attended these tournaments had a fantastic time and it helped even more to know that our fun was all for a fantastic cause.

At my financial peak, I even made enough money to buy my parents a beautiful house so they could move out of their little shack back in Erath. They had everything they needed there; a big yard, a beautiful lawn, and a house large enough to hold a real family gathering. Even with the way my father treated me, I still wanted to give my parents the best of everything. So that's what I did.

One of the greatest honors I had was being on the cover of *TV Guide* while I was on Pulpit, one of Frankie Brothers' horses. I'll never forget the looks on my kids' faces when they saw it. One day we were at the grocery store and my little Steiner poked me while she looked at the cover. She looked up at me, smiling like a small angel, and said, "Dad, look!" That moment was as surreal as it was terrific.

And if I had just kept my mouth shut, I would have had many more moments like that in my future.

But the thing was I couldn't keep my mouth shut. Even though I was at the top, there were far too many people struggling at the bottom. So I fought, not just for the sickness I felt everyday from too much reducing, but for the jockeys who were killing themselves to barely make a paycheck.

My points could have likely been heard, but again, Mr. Wayne Lukas dogged me to the media. In 2004, the *New York Times* published an article titled "Sport of the Times; Shining a Light On a Dark Side Of Life in Racing." And as always, Wayne had to drag me into his fight against jockeys.

He told the reporter, "Anything Shane Sellers says I wouldn't take too seriously. It's hard for me to feel sorry for guys who are driving three Mercedes and living in million-dollar homes and worried about six or seven pounds because they have to flip." Then to add insult to injury, he continued on to say that any jockey who didn't like the rules should "get a job washing cars or something."

Wow.

What Mr. Lukas forgot to mention to the nation when he made that statement is that only the top five or ten percent of jockeys live that sort of lifestyle. He did not point out that most riders risk their lives on an everyday basis so they can earn a $50 check. If there are ten horses in one race, only one rider has the opportunity to make what he considers serious cash. The top five finishers earn graduated payoffs, but the sixth through tenth-place riders just get the $50. That becomes about $30 after they pay their agents and valets. That's not even including the taxes they will later have to pay on that $30 they risked their lives for. So even if a rider gets the chance to be in five races one day, he's still only going to go home with about $150. And he risked his health and his life for that $150 five times.

Now I'm not too sure on the going rate for three Mercedes, but I imagine that it would take several lifetimes to afford such things with a pay of $150 a day – and that's if a jockey could live that long with all the internal damage flipping and hot boxes cause.

On top of that, every jockey is aware that the next race could be his last. We all know what can happen on the track and that's something we're willing to gamble on. Will a horse break down in front of us and cause us to crack our skulls? Will we wind up in wheelchairs if we destroy our knees? Will we be trampled to death if we fall off a horse? We can't answer any of those questions unless we are put in those situations.

But one thing we can say for sure is that we're only one jump away from death. If any of those things happen to us, the measly $100,000 insurance policies that most tracks carry for jockeys will not even come close to the enormous costs of treating traumatic injuries.

So when Mr. Lukas talks about the riches and glory of being a jockey, I would respond by saying that anything Wayne Lukas says shouldn't be taken too seriously – especially since he's driving around in three Mercedes and living in a million dollar home that he bought with our sweat.

After he made his cruel statement in the *New York Times*, several riders and I gathered together to see what we might be able to do to change things. The Kentucky Derby was quickly approaching and we all knew that anyone who placed fourth through last would get a small check that hardly made a dent in the expenses we had to pay for the privilege to ride. Not only did we have to buy tickets for our families, but our families got the worst seats at the track. They were thrown into a small area right behind the winner's circle which consisted of 100 iron folding chairs. Kelli even remembers one year when Jerry Bailey's wife had to sit on a trash can while he won the Derby on Grindstones. How ironic that they treated us like garbage and then they made our wives sit on it!

So our families would sit or stand in the most uncomfortable positions and we had to pay for that opportunity. When the races ended, anyone who placed fourth through last got a $100 check, which then became $60 after the agents and valets were paid. For the majority of us, that meant we had to pay about $940 for us and our families to be treated like trash.

For years we wondered why we couldn't wear endorsements like other professional athletes could, especially in a race as grand as the Kentucky Derby. With the exception of Suffolk Downs, every racetrack we approached gave us a firm "No!" when we brought up the endorsement question.

After years of asking nicely, we finally decided to fight the fight against Churchill Downs and take our case to court. In 2004, The Guild picked five riders to go and testify: Jerry Bailey, Jose Santos, Johnny Velasquez, Robby Albarado, and myself. We were all eager to modify the system and change the Derby forever.

On the day of our trial, I stood outside the courthouse with Jerry, Jose, Johnny, and our attorneys, waiting for the last member of our team to arrive. But alas, he never did. Robby was missing in action and the rest of us were left to fight alone.

Even though our day was off to a rough start, the rest of us were still pumped and ready to fight. Churchill's attorney opened with some arguments and then it was our turn to speak. When I got on the stand, I explained how much it cost us to ride in the Derby, along with the money we lost by leaving our other mounts back at home. My fellow jockeys and I simply explained what we went through every year at Derby time and the judge ruled in our favor.

When I walked out of the courthouse, a slew of TV cameras and microphones were thrust in my face. Churchill Downs wouldn't allow us to do any interviews on their property, so we had to do it right there. I was put in front and I got to explain our victory to everybody who was watching. The history of horse racing was changed and I was so proud to be a part of the team of four jockeys who made that happen.

All of this happened three days before the 2004 Kentucky Derby, so there was hardly any time to spare. Not only did we have to find endorsements, but we had to get their advertising patches on our outfits fast. Companies jumped on board and the phones rang off the hook. We were navigating in unchartered waters and everyone wanted a piece of the action. Within hours of hearing that we could wear endorsements, different companies overnighted us their patches. Within three days, 17 of the 18 riders in the 2004 Derby had sponsors and the opportunity to ride without paying.

Derby day was full of mayhem because there was a lot of work to be done and little time to do it. Jockeys' mothers were there, frantically sewing patches on our pants so we could have our patches ready for the big day. I've never seen so many women sew so quickly, but in the end, they pulled everything together and we all had our patches.

That year I was sponsored by Wrangler Jeans and I got $5,000 along with a box filled with a lifetime supply of jeans. We had more than enough sponsors to help every rider. Even Robby Albarado got $5,000 and a Louisville Slugger patch, despite the fact that he didn't show up at court. The only rider in the race who didn't wear a patch that year was Pat Day because he simply didn't want one.

All of us who participated in that historic day got to wear one patch from one company. It didn't matter how large the patch was, so long as it could fit on one pant leg. We couldn't go out there looking like human billboards like NASCAR drivers, but that was fine with us. One endorsement was all we needed and we were proud to display our patches that day.

Throughout my career, I rode in 14 consecutive Kentucky Derbies, but I think the 2004 Derby is the one that will always stand out in my mind. The excitement in the air was electrifying and that's one Derby that will be written into the history books.

I placed fifth in that race on Cliff's Edge, but that was fine by me. Cliff's Edge gave it his all and so did I. And unlike other Derbies, the point of this race was not simply to win, even though that would have been a nice bonus. The point was that we were all winners before we even left the starting gate.

Chapter 21

It's strange how right when you feel like you're on top of the world, someone always seems to come along and pull the world out from under you. But that's the way things happen and that's certainly what happened to me when I thought things just couldn't get any better.

After I made my comeback and I was moving up the racing ranks, I got an unexpected phone call from my brother. Since I didn't talk to my family all that often, I knew something must have been wrong. And once I heard what the estranged voice on the other side of the phone had to say, I knew my gut feeling was right.

Apparently I hadn't done enough for my father yet, and he wanted more. It wasn't enough that I bought him a beautiful house that was perfect for him and my mom. He didn't appreciate that gesture at all. He let the lawn grow until it looked wild and refused to mow it. I even went out and bought him a nice riding lawnmower to make his job easier and he still wouldn't cut the grass. Instead, he would call me and threaten, "If you don't get someone to come over here and cut this grass …"

I would say, "Dad, if you don't cut the grass, they're going to fine you."

He would laugh that gruff laugh of his and say, "Then you'd better get someone over here to take care of it fast." With that, he would hang up.

I was used to those kinds of conversations because that was how my father was. Rude. Hateful. But the day I got a call from my brother with my father's newest message, I almost had to clean out my ears to make sure I was hearing correctly.

The riding lawnmower I bought my dad had a problem and it needed to be fixed. My father wasn't willing to pay the $20 or $30 it would take to fix it, so he decided that was my responsibility. Not only was it my responsibility; it was my duty. And when I told him to just get it fixed because I was nowhere near home, it appeared that I crossed a line with the crazy old man.

With all I had done for him over the years, my dad had the balls to tell my brother, "You tell your brother I want out of this house. I want a new trailer, a truck for me, and a car for his mama."

Then he pushed things one step further when he said, "I want out of this house or I'm gonna go to the National Enquirer and tell all the trainers that he does drugs. Then I'm gonna tell his wife that he's been sleeping with all her friends."

When I heard that, I was so mad I was steaming. After all the money I gave him or he stole from me for all those years, he still couldn't get enough. And if I didn't give in to his insane demands, he was going to blackmail me with lies.

That was the breaking point for me. I thought back on everything my father had done to me throughout my life and I could feel my blood start to boil. And at that very moment, I started thinking of things I tried to block from my memory for years.

When I was 15 years old, I went out with an 18-year-old woman and started my first young, but serious relationship. She got kicked out of her house and my father said she could stay with us. After a few months, the most unexpected thing happened – she found out she was pregnant. By that point I was only 16 and our relationship was rapidly coming to an end. But still, I wanted to do the right thing and take care of our baby.

When I found out she was in labor, I rushed down to the hospital, but she didn't want me there. In fact, she never wanted me to be anywhere. As hard as I tried, she wouldn't let me meet my son. It took five long years before I got to meet him and she treated me like the devil the whole time I was there with him. When I told her that I wanted to be a part of our child's life, she finally snapped. She shouted out, "He's not yours, Shane!"

I looked at her in confusion. Of course he was mine. She lived with me when she got pregnant and I was her boyfriend at the time. I reassured myself, "Of course he was mine."

But then she said the last thing I ever expected to hear. She said, "He's not yours, Shane. He's your daddy's."

I sat there for the longest time with her words echoing in my head. My father? My father?! I knew the kind of man my father was. He stole from me. He beat my mother. He sat back and let King die. He let us *all* die on the inside. But for some reason, him cheating on my mama with my girlfriend was the last thing I expected.

As the years went on, I saw my son every now and then. We spent some time together and he knew I was his father. And man, he's enough to make any father proud. But every time I saw him and every time I think of him, I still have to wonder whether he's my son or my brother.

That's the kind of torture my father has made me live with and I had finally had enough. I wasn't going to let him treat me that way anymore. I was done.

I called my brothers and sister and told them to go get my mama out of the house. My father always said that if my mom ever left he would kill her, so I needed her to get out of there fast. I never wanted things to go this far with my father, but he more than crossed a line and I was going to turn him in to the police. I said to my siblings, "Get mama out of there. Take her cause he's going."

When the news got back to him, he was livid because he didn't want to go back to jail. He spent some time there when I was a kid and he didn't want to go back. But even as much as he wanted to stay out of jail, he still couldn't suck up his pride and try to make amends for any of the things he had done.

I called my father and asked him, "Hey, what did you say you want to do to me?"

He replied, "Call me back in ten minutes."

Again, I wanted to clean out my ears to make sure I was hearing him correctly. I said, "I ain't giving you ten minutes. You're going to jail, buddy. That's your ass."

Guided by the resentment I felt towards him for so many years, I continued, "That house you live in? I bought it for you. It's paid for. What do you want from me, man? Now you wanna blackmail me and ruin my relationship with my wife and ruin my career? For what, man? Now this is your last chance." And with that, I hung up the phone.

Never one to stop his actions until everyone around him is miserable, my father called my little sister and told her he was lying down with a rope around his neck. He said to Kristy, "See what your brother made me do?" My father had a little rope burn around his neck and he made my sister go there to see it. He showed her where he went to hang himself and tried to scare her into making me back off.

My father has been an asshole like that for as long as I can remember. That's the kind of thing he did to us as a family and to me as a person. He didn't care about anyone – including himself – and he made us remember that fact as often as possible.

Throughout the years, I pushed my pride to the side and let my father have his way. I didn't do it for him; I did it for the rest of the family. I didn't want to upset Keith, Ryan, Kristy, or above all else, my mama, so I always bit my tongue and let my father have what he wanted.

But with what he was doing now, I wasn't going to give in like I always did. Enough was enough. I had to call the police and have my daddy put in jail. Do you know how hard that is to do to your own flesh and blood; to your own father? That was one of the hardest things I've ever had to do, but it was something that had to be done.

With him gone, my mother could finally have a chance at a normal life. She wouldn't have to worry about the beatings and the yelling and the constant humiliation. She wouldn't have to be scared that she had driven too far when she went out and my father checked the odometer when she got home. She could just start over and act like she had never wasted so many years with that womanizing, abusive bastard. Things could finally be different for her and she could have a better life. In other words, she could have all the things I always thought she deserved.

So on the day that my father ripped out the last shred of respect I had for him as a father, I called the police and had him picked up. I got on a plane and went back home to deal with the situation properly. Since my father had supposedly tried to commit suicide, an ambulance came and then I had the opportunity to press charges on him. And as bad as I felt about it, I pressed charges on him so we could all finally be free of his wrath.

Soon after, I had to go to court and face my father in front of the judge. I didn't make my brothers and sister or anybody else come in with me because I didn't want to put them through that. I knew what my dad was capable of and I knew that the second anyone else saw him, they would feel bad and want to let him go. But I knew that was the worst thing we could do, so I chose to go it alone.

hardest things I've ever had to do, but it was something that had to be done.

With him gone, my mother could finally have a chance at a normal life. She wouldn't have to worry about the beatings and the yelling and the constant humiliation. She wouldn't have to be scared that she had driven too far when she went out and my father checked the odometer when she got home. She could just start over and act like she had never wasted so many years with that womanizing, abusive bastard. Things could finally be different for her and she could have a better life. In other words, she could have all the things I always thought she deserved.

So on the day that my father ripped out the last shred of respect I had for him as a father, I called the police and had him picked up. I got on a plane and went back home to deal with the situation properly. Since my father had supposedly tried to commit suicide, an ambulance came and then I had the opportunity to press charges on him. And as bad as I felt about it, I pressed charges on him so we could all finally be free of his wrath.

Soon after, I had to go to court and face my father in front of the judge. I didn't make my brothers and sister or anybody else come in with me because I didn't want to put them through that. I knew what my dad was capable of and I knew that the second anyone else saw him, they would feel bad and want to let him go. But I knew that was the worst thing we could do, so I chose to go it alone.

When the doors opened, my father came out wearing an orange jumpsuit and shackles on his feet. As he walked towards me, he looked at me and said, "I love you, son." I knew what he was doing. I knew he was trying to manipulate me. But that didn't make it hurt any less. My father had never told me he loved me before that moment and I was sure that at that moment he hated me more than he ever had before.

The whole experience killed me on the inside.

As hard as it was, I still forced myself to go up on the stand and testify against my father. I said, "I love my dad, but for him to do something like that is just taking it too far." Then I talked about some of the other things that he had done to my family and me throughout my life and I just let it all out.

In the end, my father was sent to jail and then to a mental institution. He was a sick man and the court could see that. Now all I could do was hope that maybe my father would see that, too, so we could eventually be a real family.

Chapter 22

Most professional athletes are ruled by governing bodies that want to make sure their stars are happy. They receive large paychecks, health benefits for both them and their families, retirement packages, workman's compensation, and everything else a worker in any industry could ever hope for. But since jockeys lack any unifying power and we are considered independent contractors, we weren't entitled to any of those things. And the reason we didn't have any of those things is that because unlike other athletes, we couldn't band together to fight for what we wanted.

At the peak of my career, only five states in the country offered workman's comp to jockeys. Five states! Every other state had a measly $100,000 insurance policy that only applied to track accidents. A track accident can easily cost at least $250,000 in medical bills, so that money would not go very far. The industry had nothing to offer all the jockeys who developed life-threatening medical conditions like diabetes, hypertension, and organ failure from reducing, either. So unless we jockeys rode in a workman's comp state, we were basically screwed if we suffered from more than a scraped elbow.

I was always aware of the low insurance coverage, as was the Guild. We all knew that we were being cheated and that the rules were unfair. One guy could be making the same amount of money as me and doing the same job as me, but his coverage could have been the difference between life and death – all because of a state line.

It just wasn't right and all of us knew it.

But even with our knowledge, our predicament didn't really hit home until a kid named Gary Birzer was in a horrible accident in a non-workman's comp state. He was riding in West Virginia at Mountaineer Race racetrack when he fell off his horse. The crowd must have heard the loud crack when he smashed into the ground as he injured his spinal column and became instantly paralyzed from the waist down.

The sound of his injury reverberated to every jocks' room while we tuned into the news as Gary's story got worse and worse. When Gary fell, he thought he was riding on a one million dollar insurance policy. He didn't realize that the Guild had reduced that policy years before and that he, like the rest of us, was only riding on a $100,000 policy.

As his medical bills piled up, Gary realized that $100,000 doesn't really go all that far. I would be surprised if that money even covered his first week in the hospital. The Jockey's Guild had a fund set aside for disabled riders, but that didn't help Gary like it was supposed to. Instead, Gary and his wife Amy were stuck paying the bills by themselves.

Soon his bills amounted to almost a million dollars and there was no way he could afford his medical expenses. He was basically kicked out of the hospital because he couldn't pay and nearly every rehab center turned him down, as well.

Gary's life became a living nightmare. Not only did he lose the ability to walk, ride, or do any other physical activities, but he lost the ability to care for his family. For the rest of us jockeys who could do nothing but sit by and watch, we saw our worst fears manifest themselves through this poor man who had sacrificed everything just so he could ride.

After Gary's accident, everybody became paranoid. Every time I saw a horse stumble, I was scared that I was going to lose everything I had, too. What if the same thing happened to me? How would I take care of Kelli, Shali, Saban, and Steiner? What would I do if I couldn't ride and my wife had to support our family like my mother supported her family when we were growing up?

All of these questions floated around my head, infecting me with the negative answers to all of them. If I ever suffered an injury like Gary's, I wouldn't be able to do anything. It was that simple.

At that point, I couldn't help but wonder what kept me in the game, anyway. I had a great career. I had now won over 4,000 races. My wife and kids were comfortable. I had wonderful friends and a fantastic family all of whom I loved deeply. Really, I had everything I needed.

Still, I couldn't shake my desire for the thrill of the game and all that came with it.

So I kept riding with all of these thoughts in mind. I tried to ignore the pain I still suffered from my knee injury and the fear I felt from Gary's spill. Trying to stay strong, I rode in a stakes race at Turfway Park in Kentucky, and I was ready to board a private plane to fly to Hoosier Park in Anderson, Indiana to ride in the Indiana Derby. But as I sat on that plane, I didn't want to go. I was afraid and I didn't want to risk everything when I knew that I was riding on a $100,000 policy. I didn't have it in me. For the first time in my life, I put my logic before my dreams and I just didn't want to go.

I thought back on how many times I had hit the ground and how fearless I tried to remain through all of it. I thought of all of my friends and fellow riders who had been hurt – Robby had a metal plate in his head, Gary was paralyzed and in a wheelchair, Randy's kidneys were eaten up, and Chris Herrell and Emanuel Jose Sanchez were dead. All of these men – all of my friends – had put themselves in the same position I put myself in every day and they paid a serious price.

Aside from my love for racing, why had I always been willing to pay such a price? For my family. I didn't want my family to grow up hungry like I did. I wanted my kids to have everything they wanted. I wanted them to go to college and have wonderful lives. I wanted to buy Kelli tokens of my affection and remind her of how much I loved her. I wanted to do all of that – and by that point I had accomplished all of it.

So now the reason that I wanted to ride was the same reason I didn't want to ride – my family.

After a lot of thinking, I sat Kelli down the same way I sat her down when I told her how much I wanted to go back to riding after my knee injury. But this time I felt like a kid begging his

202

mother to please let him miss a day of school or quit a sports team. I explained all of my fears to her. I told her everything that was on my mind. Ever understanding, Kelli didn't need me to justify my fears. She was scared by what I went through, too.

Holding onto her hands, I said, "Kelli, our kids are growing up and I want to be there to see them grow more. I don't want to go out like Gary did; I don't want to leave you all with nothing. We might have to cut back on our lifestyle a bit, but we have enough money to live on with what we've saved. This lifestyle isn't me, anyway."

Kelli gripped my hands harder and looked me in the eye while she replied, "Baby, I'm always here for you. Whatever you want to do is the right decision; I'm going to support you."

A rush of relief flowed through my body when she said that. As long as Kelli understood, I didn't need to justify my decision to anybody else. Feeling more at peace than I had in a long time, I told Kelli, "I'm gonna ride the stakes race I'm already booked for and that's going to be my last race. Whatever I make, I'm going to donate to Gary. That's my incentive. And then I'm never gonna ride under this $100,000 insurance policy ever again." With Kelli's support and my own determination, that was the decision I made.

On the day of my last race, I went to the jocks' room and told the reporters that it was the last day I was going to ride. I publicly announced, "I'm not retiring, but this is the last race I'm going to ride with a $100,000 policy." I saw all of the shocked faces around me with people's jaws almost touching the floor. Then I made the final comment, "This race is for Gary Birzer and anything I might win is going towards his medical expenses."

Judging by the looks on everyone's faces, I could see they knew I meant business.

Later in the day, some jockeys tried to talk me out of my decision. Tony D'Amico came up to me and said, "Shane, man. What are you doing?"

Tony was a great friend of mine, but I had to stand firm. I looked Tony square in the eye and said, "Tony, it's gonna happen again. It's only a matter of time."

I tried to explain my feelings and fears to all of the jockeys in the room, but they just weren't listening. My hotheaded side came out and I started raising my voice. They knew as well as I did that this wouldn't be the last time that we would see one of our brothers go down in a blaze of pain and medical bills. But they weren't listening to what I was saying; they didn't want to hear it. Or maybe they just weren't mentally ready to think about it. In any case, all of my words fell on deaf ears.

Knowing that my fellow jockeys weren't going to back me up on this move, I left the jock's room and rode my last race. Unfortunately, I didn't win, so all my hopes of giving Gary a hefty check were nothing more than wishful thinking.

Even though I felt discouraged that day, I knew a day would come when my friends would be ready to make more changes in the industry. It was only a matter of time before someone else suffered from the same fate as Gary and I knew that my jockey friends might finally take a stand when it happened.

In the meantime, I packed up my things and said my goodbyes. The day got even harder when I had to approach Steve Asmussen and my agent Fred Aime to tell them my plans. Steve resurrected my career after my injury and now I had to walk up to him and tell him my decision. He said, "Whenever you're ready to come back, I understand." And when I heard the leaning trainer say that, I almost didn't want to walk out the door.

But I did walk out the door and I didn't look back. I made my decision just like that and I stopped riding. From that moment on, I didn't talk to a single jockey. I didn't talk to anybody about racing, about weights, about insurance, about anything. I just returned to my roots and waited for the day when I could return to a better industry that would care for me as much as I cared for it.

Part 4

From Hero
To Asshole

Chapter 23

Fishing is a lot like riding a bicycle. You can go months, years, or even decades without doing it, but once the rod is in your hand, it's like you never left the lake.

When I went home after my last race, that's exactly how I felt. I suddenly had time to do things that I hadn't done for years. I got to spend time with Kelli and our kids, bonding with them over family barbeques, throwing a ball around, or even sitting down to eat a dinner that I could actually digest. I had the chance to spend more time with my closest friends outside of the hot box. I even had the opportunity to start fishing and hunting again, which were always two of my favorite pastimes. Basically, I got to do a lot of things once my schedule wasn't jammed with heaving, sweating, riding, and playing political Jeopardy.

About two months went by and I hadn't heard from any of the jockeys except for some of my closest friends. I didn't get a single phone call from a jockey, a trainer, or an owner, even though we practically all lived together up until two months earlier. It was a little discouraging, but at the same time it was relieving. Now I could see who my true friends were and set my priorities in order.

One night I went out to a karaoke bar and I drank and sang until the wee hours of the morning. Kelli and I had been fighting and I tried to drain my sorrows in booze and song. I drank way more than I should have that night and I stayed at my friend Mark Guidry's house for the night, waiting for my inevitable hangover.

My cell phone rang at what felt like the crack of dawn and I expected it to be Kelli. With my head still spinning and my voice still slurred, I picked up the phone and said, "Hello?"

I didn't expect to be greeted by the voice of a jockey who I hadn't spoken to in months. In his thick Spanish accent, one of the riders said, "Papi, we're having a meeting at Churchill and we need you to come."

Still as drunk as I had been the night before, I asked the simple question, "Why? What's going on?"

He proceeded to tell me that Tony D'Amico had fallen and that his medical bills were already up to $250,000 after one week in the hospital. The rest of the jockeys finally had a wake-up call and they wanted my help to raise the insurance policies.

I couldn't believe what I was hearing. Two months earlier I told them that this would happen again, but they didn't want to listen. Gary Birzer's accident wasn't enough for them. They needed to wait until Tony got hurt, too.

And even though they forgot that I existed from the moment I said I'm not riding until the insurance goes up, they still called on me. Why? Because they knew I would stand up like I did every other time. Just like with the weights and the endorsements, they knew I would stand up for them. It was in my nature to stand up for the guys who couldn't – or wouldn't – stand up for themselves and this situation was no different than the others.

Trying to keep my brain from throbbing out of my hungover skull, I got up, threw my clothes on, and headed over to

Churchill Downs. I walked into the jocks' room with my drunken logic guiding me while I tried to make sense of the whole situation.

The jockeys told me they were having a meeting with track management. They wanted to do what they had done for the Breeders' Cup, which meant they wanted to go on strike if the insurance policy wasn't raised. The problem was that what they did with the Breeders' Cup wasn't a permanent solution. The jockeys told management that they wouldn't ride without a half million dollar policy. They got the half million they wanted, but it only lasted for one day. The next day, they were riding for $100,000 again.

Before that happened, another jockey named Gary Boulanger fell and he fell hard. When his body slammed into the ground, two horses trampled over him. As a result, Gary was left with a ruptured spleen, a subdural hematoma, and a stack of medical bills bigger than the horses that ran him over. But as bad as Gary's injuries were, they still weren't bad enough to make the riders want a permanent change yet.

When Tony D'Amico fell, it just went to show the third time is a charm. It took three riders to nearly get killed with $100,000 policies backing them before the rest of the jockeys were ready to take serious action.

So now there they were and they wanted to finally make some permanent changes. Their actions before the Breeders' Cup showed them the power they had, but they still waited all that time to band together and fight. It was about to be show time, and they had no idea of how to get what they wanted.

Happy that the jockeys were finally ready for change, but annoyed that they forgot I existed until that epiphany struck them, I told them I would help. Before the meeting, I addressed all the jocks and said, "You've got two choices: You either ride or don't ride." I grabbed a piece of paper, wrote my name on it, and told everyone else who wasn't going to ride to put their names down, too.

The piece of paper made its way around the jock's room, but a lot of jockeys were still hesitant to sign. Once almost everyone had signed, the rest of the jockeys were nervous because it was Pat Day's turn to make his decision and he was always loyal to Churchill Downs. When I saw that nobody else was making a move, I had to physically walk up to Pat Day, slam the piece of paper on the table in front of him, and say, "C'mon Little Jesus. Are you gonna sign or not?" Without saying a word, Pat put his signature on that piece of paper. With everyone's signatures in place, I knew we had a consensus.

I addressed everyone in the room and said, "You have a $100,000 policy. I'm telling you this now and I told you back then. This is what you got. After $100,000, you're responsible for the rest."

Then I turned to the Spanish guys in the room and said, "You sabe?" I looked around at them and said, "If he don't sabe, make him sabe."

At that point, some executives from the track walked into the room and I addressed them, too. I said, "I was called down here for a meeting and I just found out why. These guys are uncomfortable with their insurance policies and they want something better."

With the members of management still there listening, I turned to the jockeys and said, "Right now you have two choices. You can keep riding on your $100,000 policy or you can stop riding. The third choice that you came up with is to ask management for a half million dollar policy, but you have a better chance of flying in a hot air balloon than that happening. I'm not telling you what to do. That's a choice you all have to make for yourselves. I'm just telling you as a Guild rep what your choices are."

Now feeling more irritated that they called me down there to begin with, I continued, "I'm gonna pray for you. That's all I can do. If you want, you can do what I do. I ain't comfortable with the policy, so I ain't riding."

That was all I had to say, so I left the room. Some of the jockeys tried to stop me, but I just said, "I'll see y'all later," as I walked out the door.

As it turned out, I did see them all later and that was the second big mistake I made that day.

Chapter 24

When you're a kid, a clubhouse is the ultimate sign of power. You can pick and choose who can enter, who can play, and who can only stand outside, wishing they were cool enough to get in. Well, I didn't have a clubhouse when I was a kid, but I had the chance to go in a lot of clubhouses when I got older.

We jockeys may have been grown men, but we still liked to do our business in the confines of a clubhouse.

After the jockeys finished their meeting with management and the races ended for the day, I went back to Mark Guidry's "clubhouse" with them to talk. They all wanted to strike; to stand outside Churchill Downs with picket signs and do a group chant. Normally, I would have been the first to join them. But by that point, my "Hell no, we won't go" kind of mentality had faded. I had already taken my stance and I didn't want to get involved any more than I already was.

I sat there and listened while everyone talked about who was going to strike and who wasn't going to ride. Within a few hours, everyone stood firm on their decisions to make a permanent change. Our clubhouse meeting was adjourned and I was free to get back to my new life.

Unfortunately, the jocks weren't ready to let me do that just yet. The next morning, my phone rang again and I learned that there was another meeting in the jock's room. So I went to the track and got there around 10:00 in the morning because that's the time when jockeys usually finished their workouts.

Calvin was sitting there, wrapped in a towel and fixing to go make weight. Robby was there getting ready for his mounts. I was sitting at the counter with Rafael Bejarano, eating a bowl of soup together. He was the leading rider in Kentucky, but he told me that he was leaving for New York. That was a way for him to avoid striking with the rest of the bunch. He was going to a workman's comp state so he wouldn't have to worry about what would happen if he had an accident, and I didn't blame him.

While we were still sitting at the counter, two guys walked directly over to me. I recognized one of them as a security guard, but the other one was dressed in plain clothes. The guard I knew asked me, "Shane, do you have any mounts today?"

Considering how long it had been since I last rode, I was sure he knew the answer to that question, but I still responded "No."

When he heard my answer, he told me that I had to leave the property. I knew that wasn't right. Even if you don't have any mounts, you're allowed to stay in the jocks' room until noon. I knew the rules. I also knew that my jockey friend Jose Martinez was standing there next to me and he didn't have any mounts that day, either. He even told that to the guards.

Well aware of what was and was not allowed, I told the security guard, "I'm a rider. I know my rights."

He looked right back at me and said, "You need to leave the premises."

Shocked, I asked him, "Are you serious?"

He responded, "Yeah, you need to leave right now."

I couldn't believe what was happening. I was at home minding my own business and the jockeys had called me in for another meeting. Then I was minding my own business while I ate my soup and I was being kicked out. The situation was absurd and I couldn't understand the reason for it.

Why did my fellow jockeys call me in that day? Did they plan for me to get kicked out? Or was it Churchill Downs that had it in for me? What the hell was going on and why was I dragged into the middle of it?

With all of those questions still running through my mind, I told the security guard, "Alright, you'll never see me on another horse again." Still unsure of who had set this up, I looked around at everyone in the room and repeated, "You'll never see me on another horse again in my entire life."

There wasn't time for a speech, though, so I had to move right along. I told the security guards that Kentucky was my home track and that all of my tack was still there. I asked if I could get it and they told me that would be fine.

I felt so angry at that moment that all I could do was swear and raise my voice. I just kept repeating, "You'll never see me ride again, you sorry motherfuckers."

As my voice got louder, Calvin got out of the hot box wrapped in his towel and asked, "Shane, what the hell is going on?" Soon after, Robby came out and all of the other riders congregated around me, trying to figure out what was happening.

Calvin was as outraged as I was as he handed me a bag and the guards were pushing me to leave as quickly as possible. All I wanted was to get my things from my locker, but it was locked. My valet had the key, and he wasn't there that day, so I couldn't get in to get my tack. The guard didn't want to wait for me to get to my stuff. In fact, he was so adamant about me leaving that he threatened to have me arrested if I didn't get out of there right away.

Feeling angrier than I could ever remember feeling, I said, "Someone get somebody on the phone. These people are throwing me off the track. You guys called me in here. Someone tell me what is going on." The guys got the Guild on the phone and told them what was going on. I spoke to a man named Darryl Haire and told him everything that had happened over the past two days. He listened to my story and said, "Listen, you get your tack and if they put handcuffs on you, we'll see them in court."

So I hung up to get my stuff and about five minutes later the security guards came over to me again. Calvin and I were almost finished packing my belongings. In five more minutes, we would have been done.

Apparently five minutes wasn't good enough for the guards. One of them said, "You need to leave or we're going to put the handcuffs on you, Shane." Then before I knew it, they took out a pair of handcuffs and yelled for me to turn around. At that split second, I didn't know if I was going to hit the guard or turn around. I was beyond thinking and I felt that I had nothing else to lose. If I was going to go to jail, I was going to go for something other than eating a bowl of soup in the wrong place at the wrong time.

That was when I heard Willie Martinez shout out, "No, man! Don't put no handcuffs on him!" When he saw that I was either going to get cuffed or get arrested for a good reason, he pleaded, "Please Shane. Please Papi. Don't do anything."

And that was the only reason I turned around. With my face turned towards the bench, I heard the loud click of the cuffs being secured. The handcuffs felt cold against my skin in sharp contrast to the blood that boiled within my veins.

With tears rolling down my cheeks, I went to walk over to my bag on the floor, but the security guard yanked me backwards. Feeling more degraded than ever, I yelled out, "Hey, dude!"

He snidely responded, "Two seconds ago you didn't want to move. Now slow down."

I was so angry that I could have killed someone at that very moment. Why in God's name was this happening to me?

When the guards started to walk away with me, Calvin came down the stairs in his towel and said, "What the fuck are you guys doing?"

Someone else yelled, "Shane don't do nothing crazy!"

I was so angry that I didn't know what to do with myself. Two men had cuffed me and all I could hear was, "Shane, now don't go crazy." That's easier said than done, my friend. Those guys called me down there and they could do nothing but watch while I was cuffed like a common criminal.

Not one to fight a cause that couldn't be won, I left with the guards. I curbed my impulse to swing or flail and I let them cuff me right in the jock's room. Still hearing the riders in the background, I hung my head in shame while I walked towards the guards' destination.

I just sat back and took it, much like the outraged jockeys who watched me leave even though *they* were the ones who called me there.

Cowards.

Sure, they were angry because of what happened to me. But they were also angry about the jockey weight limits. They were also angry that we could not wear endorsements. They were also angry that we had to risk our lives with minimal insurance policies.

But as angry as they were about all of these things, they continued to sit back and ignore what was happening around them while they drowned their consciences in their metaphorical bowls of soup.

Of course, a few of the jockeys tried to back me at the time, but I was still angry. My thoughts were all over the place; my brain was scrambled. I was looking at the riders, mad at the riders, mad at management, mad at the Guild. I was mad at everyone and everything because all I had been doing was eating a bowl of soup.

My lack of guilt didn't matter, though. The two security guards each took an arm and led me outside. The jockeys followed me out there, some wearing nothing but their towels, while they shouted out words of support that I couldn't even understand.

The guards continued to guide me down their chosen path and we ended up in the security office. They closed the doors behind us and one security guard turned to me and said, "Between you, me, and these walls, I understand."

Well, gee, that was helpful.

The guards were going to arrest me, but they said they would talk to management. The kinder of the guards said, "Just let me let you walk out of here. We'll take the cuffs off, you can go to your car, and you can go. I won't arrest you."

I looked at him and asked the easiest question in the world. "What did I do wrong?"

He responded, "Shane, I understand you. I understand your cause. But I gotta do my job. I've known you since you've been here, but I gotta do my job." When he saw the defeated look on my face, he continued, "I'm gonna talk to management and say that you didn't put up a fight. I'll tell them not to press any charges."

And even though he understood, his words still jerked me. The guards saw the riders follow me out; they saw their passion. I wasn't there because I wanted to be. I was invited. I was asked to come.

I had been there the day before and that wasn't a problem. Nobody cared that I didn't have any mounts, nor did they care that I showed up for the first jockey meeting. Nobody told me that I wasn't welcome and what would happen if I responded to my invitation the next day. If I had known then what I know now, I never would have gone to the meeting in the first place.

But the power of retrospect doesn't help when it comes to a situation like this. I didn't know what was in store for me and I could have never predicted what would happen next. All I knew was that the walk from the security office to my car was the longest, loneliest walk I had ever taken. I could see the guys standing there with their heads down, staring at the ground and trying not to look at what was happening in front of them. Even though I knew their thoughts were with me, I still knew I was alone.

And as lonely as I felt that day, I didn't even know the meaning of loneliness – yet.

Chapter 25

A day may not seem that long, but it really is if you think about it. One day lasts for 24 hours, 1,440 minutes, or 86,400 seconds. On the day that I was handcuffed and thrown out of Churchill Downs, every second seemed to last an eternity.

When I left Churchill Downs, I didn't know what to do with myself. I was devastated about my situation, but I knew that there was another person who was going through something even worse than I was. So wiping my tears away, I drove straight to the hospital to visit Tony D'Amico because I knew he was in need. His finances were in shambles and he couldn't afford the help he needed.

Before I walked into the hospital room, Tony's wife came over to me at the doorway. She said, "Tony won't let them work on his shoulder." Tony's shoulder had completely shattered and he was too concerned about the money to even let them help him. His wife looked like she was going to break down in tears again as she started talking about all the bills and about their money concerns in general.

I walked over to Tony's bedside and leaned down to give him a hug. I was extra gentle with him because his rib cage had collapsed and it was crushing down on his lungs. The doctors had to give him a tracheotomy so he could still breathe.

Looking down at my good friend, I said, "Tony, man," and he looked at me with the saddest face I had ever seen. When he said that he couldn't get the surgery because he needed money to take care of his wife and kids, I wanted to start crying all over again.

With my voice shaking, I said, "Don't worry about it, man. We'll get the money. We'll find a way. Just let the doctors go in there and fix your shoulder up. Even if I have to pay for it myself, we'll get it for you, Tony. Just relax, let them fix you, and we'll take care of this."

In a hoarse voice, Tony replied, "You told me. I should have listened to you."

I said, "Tony, don't even say that. That's not why I came here. I came to say hello to you and to let you know I love you, brother."

Lost in his thoughts, Tony repeated himself and said, "You told us. You said it."

Ignoring what I had said in the past and all of the animosity that I felt towards what was going on because of the insurance issue now, I replied, "You know, you'll get by this and we'll be fine. You're breathing man, and that's the main thing."

After that, there was nothing much to say. Tony and I sat there in silence while his wife continued to stand in the doorway. Both of us thought over our respective situations and I think at that moment I felt as helpless as he did.

For the life of me, I couldn't understand why any of this was happening. I didn't know what Tony did to deserve that kind of pain and I didn't know what I did wrong, either. Truth be told, I still don't.

I went to Churchill Downs two days in a row. The first day I was there for about a half hour and the second day I was there for about 20 minutes. What could I have possibly done that was so bad in less than an hour combined?

I don't know what I did, but I can tell you what I sure didn't do. I didn't stand in front of Churchill Downs holding a picket sign the next day. I didn't cause a public display of my distaste for management. I didn't broadcast my qualms with the low insurance policies on a sign. I didn't do any of those things. But 17 other riders did and I was somehow grouped with them.

While the jockeys picketed, they were brought inside to talk to management. In an intimidating effort to make the guys back down, management split them into two groups rather than letting them speak as a whole like any legitimate union is supposed to be able to do.

That intimidation tactic certainly worked because nobody in one group knew what the people in the other group were saying. Did they give up the fight? Did they blame the people in the other group to save themselves? Or did they stand firm and make the same demands they made when the group was all together? Nobody knew the answers to those questions, so it was very easy for management to scare the riders.

When the two groups were finally reunited, nobody knew who was going to ride. Sure, there was a piece of paper that said nobody would ride, but that paper didn't mean anything. In the end, Pat Day decided to take Churchill's advice and ride, despite the fact that he had etched his signature on that paper just like everyone else. Nobody made him sign it; he signed it with the free will God gave him. But since Pat was such a big shot at Churchill, everyone in his group decided that they would ride with him, too.

So the races went on, and Pat Day was the leader of his pack. He, the midgets, and the scabs who chose to stay with him kept the races going. The other 17 riders – 18 if you included me – were ruled off for the rest of the meet. We weren't allowed to ride at Churchill. I don't know about the rest of the riders, but I wasn't allowed to ride at Arlington Park or any other property that Churchill Downs owned, either.

The banned riders were none too pleased to be ruled off because their careers – their very livelihoods – depended on racing. I wasn't too concerned for myself because I had already gone over two months without riding. And even though I still wasn't willing to ride with the current policy, I was utterly annoyed that the riders who dragged me into their battle never called me again after they went on strike.

A couple weeks before the Kentucky Derby, I heard that the other 17 riders were reinstated, so I assumed that I had been, too. I was thrilled because I wanted to get back to work for Steve Asmussen and pick up where I had left off. But a week later, I got a letter in the mail from Churchill's management. I tore it open to read it and when I finished reading, the piece of white paper slipped out of my hands and fluttered onto the floor.

At that moment, I could feel my face turn as white as that sheet of paper while all the blood drained out of me. The letter said that I was still barred from the racetrack and that I couldn't be anywhere on the premises. Not as a rider, not as a spectator.

Churchill Downs threw me out faster than Romeo was banished from Verona after he killed Tybalt. The management looked me in the eye and basically said, "Shane – thou art banished."

And banished I was.

I could never set foot on Churchill Downs' property again. I could not compete in what would have been my 15th consecutive Kentucky Derby. I couldn't even get close enough to the property to *watch* the Derby.

But the rest of the riders who called me into this were going to ride with a million dollar policy that my sacrifice helped them get. These same riders who didn't listen when I originally suggested that we strike, these same riders who didn't call me for two months, these same riders who *begged* me to help them … These same riders who I *thought* were my friends.

It wasn't just the riders, though. It was also Churchill and the Guild itself. In the brief time that I was outside with handcuffs, some kid recorded the whole incident on his camera phone. At the time, I didn't even know that the worst moment of my life was all captured on film.

The next day, the Jockey's Guild flew in the president to help me and try to get my good name back. Kelli and I put him up in our house and we cooked him a nice steak dinner. Then he said, "We've got a limo and we're going to go to all the TV stations. Some kid had a recorder phone and taped the whole thing. We're splicing it."

He put me in a limo and drove me to four different TV stations. At the first station, they took a chunk of the tape, spliced it, and put it on a reel. I watched them do the whole thing. Then they just took the tape and let all the other TV stations use it.

The Guild president and I went from station to station, and everybody played that damn tape for the world to see. I just sat next to him, trying not to cry while they showed me being hauled off in handcuffs. I basically sat there and said, "Ya know, I don't know what happened. The reason why they are doing what they're doing is because of insurance. I haven't been riding for two months."

There was a lot more that I wanted to say, but I couldn't. We didn't have time to get into all the details because that was not the main topic of the programs. We were there to talk about insurance in general and the footage of me being paraded around in handcuffs was just used to emphasize the serious nature of what was going on.

By the time we finished touring all the TV stations, I was embarrassed but thankful. I was grateful that the Guild president had flown all the way over to help me clear my reputation within the industry. But the truth of the matter was that he wasn't helping me; he was using me like a pawn in his little game.

I was a representative in the Guild for over 20 years and I did everything to live up to their expectations of me. I fought for all my fellow riders and I brought every one of their grievances to the Guild to see if I could help. When it came time to help me, the Guild sat back as quietly as the 17 riders they got reinstated.

My head was spinning and I just couldn't understand why this was happening to me. I didn't hold a sign; I didn't boycott Churchill Downs. I only tried to help my fellow riders who asked me to help them get better insurance policies. As a Guild rep, I knew I was as responsible for taking care of my friends as the Guild was for taking care of me.

And the riders didn't get each other back. The *Guild* got negotiated a deal to get them back. Derby time was coming and Churchill needed great riders for great horses. Nobody wanted to watch the Kentucky Derby with a bunch of scabs riding, so the Guild, the track, and the outside people did what they had to do.

The only problem was that they completely forget to put me back in the equation. They didn't even try to get me reinstated with the other riders. The governor had stepped in at that point and said, "You got a million dollar insurance policy, you got people's attention, people understand what happened, so now you can get back to riding."

To make matters better, or worse, depending on your perspective, the governor even began a motion to let Kentucky start offering workman's comp there.

So to make a long story short, I got ruled off for eating a bowl of soup and the other 17 men got reinstated for picketing and causing a stir. I didn't stand there with them. I didn't make a sign. I didn't do anything. And still, I was the one who couldn't ride in the Derby or even get close enough to watch it.

At that time, nearly everyone took advantage of my situation and I felt terrible about it. I felt betrayed by my friends, my fellow riders, the Guild, and everyone else who was involved. I did everything they asked of me, and in the end, I was the one who paid.

I followed the Guild president from TV station to TV station, publicly embarrassing myself and my family. Do you know what it's like to be a little kid and see your daddy on TV in handcuffs? I don't know that feeling, but my kids sure do. Just like I had to face the humiliation in front of my peers, my kids had to deal with the mortification they felt in front of all their friends and teachers. And poor Kelli. She stood by me every step of the way, and she had to suffer while she walked around town with everyone pitifully looking at the lady who was married to the fool in handcuffs.

My whole family got fucked by this situation. It was not just the Guild, not just the jockeys, and not just Churchill Downs that fucked us. The entire industry stepped in and fucked me and my entire family.

They took away my pride, my honor, and my reputation. Even worse, they made me feel like a failure in front of the people I loved the most.

It took me 26 long years to reach the professional status I had earned, and just like that, I went from hero to asshole. My life as I knew it was over and I doubted that I would ever be the same again.

And as time has proven, my feeling was right.

Chapter 26

Have you ever had someone ask you to guess the answer to a question that you couldn't possibly know the answer to? You sit there, racking your brain for the right answer, and then you reach a point where you just give up. So you ask your friend to tell you the answer and they say, "Nope, you'll have to guess."

Well, that's how I felt after I was banned from Churchill. I asked everyone I knew for an answer and nobody had one. Churchill's management didn't know why I wasn't reinstated. The Guild didn't know why I wasn't reinstated. The riders didn't know why I wasn't reinstated. And since *I* sure as hell didn't know why I wasn't reinstated, each new person who basically asked me to guess made me want to rip my hair out.

The days kept coming and going, still without any answers. A lot of the jockeys came up to me one at a time and said that they had tried to talk to management. Gary Stevens and Mark Guidry both told me they tried to get me back, but they couldn't. Jose Martinez spoke to management and said he didn't have any mounts that day either and he wanted to know why I couldn't be reinstated. Even Ken Patin tried to find an answer for me, but he just couldn't get one.

And as much as I know that these individuals tried to see what the problem was, they still left me as clueless as I was when I approached the higher powers on my own.

One thing that I tried to teach the rest of the riders throughout my career was that if we stood together as a group, we could win any battle. Everyone who struck as a group got their million dollar insurance policy and they were all reinstated. If they had approached management together, I know they could have gotten me back. But just like all the other times there was a problem, nobody was willing to stand together for a common cause. Instead, they all brought it up in a casual way so they wouldn't have to jeopardize their futures like I jeopardized mine.

All I wanted to know was who dropped the ball. Who was it that hated me so much that I couldn't get reinstated? Did my friends sacrifice me so they could ride my potential mounts? Did the Guild decide to use me as a scapegoat? Or did Churchill Downs simply hate me so much that they stomped on all my dreams? Who was it? And why did they do it?

When Derby time came, I still didn't have any answers and I didn't know what to think. For 14 years in a row I had ridden in every Derby. That year, I couldn't ride and I couldn't even sit in the grandstand to watch.

Suddenly I was like that little boy from Erath who was shunned by everybody and anybody, for reasons he couldn't control.

On Derby Day, I was invited to a party in a big barn. Everybody there knew my situation and they knew what I was going through. While I sat there and watched the races, I just wanted to fall through a crack in the floor and disappear. All eyes were on me and I could feel everyone's stares. Some people looked at me with pity and others looked at me like I was a criminal. In either case, I didn't want to be pitiful or be a criminal. I was so mortified by the way people looked at me that I wanted to crawl in a hole and die.

Trying to ignore the stares and the occasional whisper of someone saying, "That poor bastard," I tried to focus on the races. There my friends were, riding with their million dollar policies, and there I was sitting in a barn. As much as I didn't want the people at the party to pity me, I knew my situation was truly pitiful.

As more days came and went, I became even more pitiful than ever. I found myself torn between screaming and crying. My mind was on a constant rollercoaster ride through Hell and I didn't know how to snap out of it. I hated myself, I hated my friends, and at times, I even hated my family. It was like all the love went out of me and all I could feel was hate.

I had always been hotheaded, but from that moment on, I found it harder to control my temper. Kelli would say something to me and I would just start yelling at her for no reason. I knew none of this was her fault, but I couldn't stop my snappy attitude. Every person and every thing made me want to kill someone. I wanted to put on the gloves my father used to throw at me and make other people feel as much pain on the outside as I felt on the inside.

Of course, I never took things to that level. I was angry, but I wasn't completely insane. All I wanted was an answer. Just one honest answer. But nobody would give me what I needed and the longer I waited to find out why I was in this predicament, the more I hated the world around me.

I started to pull away from everyone I knew. My friends, my family, everyone. I was emotionally destroyed and I didn't want to be near anyone who could either help me feel better or make me feel worse.

When my friends first called me down to Churchill Downs, I ignored the fact that they were all missing in action for the two months I didn't ride. I dropped everything, even through a hangover, and rushed to the jocks' room to see what they needed. When it came to me, though, nobody dropped anything. They either stayed away from me or acted as if nothing had changed. But everything had changed and it seemed like nobody else could see that.

My world was suddenly different and I felt like nobody else cared. So I continued lashing out at those I loved the most to hide from the person I hated the most – me.

Unaware of what I was doing at the time, I completely isolated myself from everyone and everything I loved. I didn't spend as much time with Kelli and the kids, and the time I did spend with them was filled with a lot of fighting. I didn't want to see my friends anymore and it killed me every time I had to get together with one of them, either to hang out or because they were there to visit their godchildren.

All of these riders were so deeply embedded in my life that there was no way to escape them. Jerry Bailey's son was Saban's best friend, so I knew I had to see him all the time. And it's not that I had anything against Jerry. He was and is someone I will always admire. But it was painful to be around anyone who had anything to do with my career and almost everyone in my life had something to do with my career.

There were some people like Jerry that I couldn't escape from, but I completely severed my ties with those who I could avoid seeing. I burned a lot of bridges during that time and I'll always regret that fact. However, I had been burned so badly that I just didn't care that I was pushing so many people out of my life.

I didn't know how to come to terms with the man I had become. I wasn't the happy rider anymore, nor was I the happy family man. If anything, I was becoming a bitter man like my father. As mentally ill as I felt, I would have never done the things to my wife or children that my father did to me, my mom, and my siblings. But still, I could suddenly relate to the hatred he felt towards the world.

Like Dr. Jekyll and Mr. Hyde, I was torn between acting like a man and acting like a monster. I was sick with hatred and I didn't know how to get my life back. I just felt so betrayed that I didn't know who I could and could not trust anymore. And by letting these things get to me so much, I had betrayed myself.

I grew up as a strong guy and I began to see that I wasn't nearly as strong as I thought I was. I cried myself to sleep every night and Kelli would wake me because I was either crying or yelling while I slept.

It felt like every little problem that I ever had came back to bite me in the ass during that time. I could feel the pain from every jab my father made at me with the gloves. I could visualize all of the pitying looks I got when I was a kid or when I sat at the party in that barn on Derby Day. All of these things drifted in and out of my mind, weaving themselves through my very soul, until I didn't even know who or what I was anymore.

The only thing I knew was that I wasn't the man I used to be, and I didn't like a single thing about the man I had become.

Chapter 27

As the old adage goes, "When it rains, it pours." I'd like to slap the guy who made up that sentence because it's a stupid way to explain how everything falls apart at once. But since the world has accepted that cliché, I'm going to stick with it because the sentiment behind that sentence is completely true.

When it starts to rain, it sure does pour.

Soon after I isolated myself from almost everyone I knew, I became more isolated than I ever wanted to be. My temper had taken control of me and Kelli left with the kids. At the time, I didn't have the words to tell her how much I loved her and how badly I wanted all of them back. I just let them go and sent them checks as often as I could.

At that point, I was completely alone and I never realized the true meaning of loneliness until then. But with no wife, no kids, and no friends by my side, the definition of loneliness became quite clear.

I spent my days and nights by myself, just lying on the couch and wasting away. I didn't want to hunt or fish or do anything else that I enjoyed. I just wanted to lie there and let my life pass me by.

While I was in my slump, I started getting more phone calls from my family in Louisiana than I had ever gotten before. My father had been getting help for a while and now he was ready to reenter all of our lives – if I would let him.

Soon after my father went away, I sold my parents' house and bought my mother a new trailer where she could start her life over again. I said to her, "This trailer is for you, Mama. I don't want him living here with you because you can do better than him."

My mother was really thankful and for a while it looked like she was going to start living out her life again. Suddenly she had time to spend with her friends and she could do some of the things that she hadn't been allowed to do for decades.

On the day my dad was arrested, she was really scared and we had to coax her back into living her life again. We took her to my aunt's camp in "the Basin" and the only way to get there was by boat. My mama was terrified even though we couldn't have been going more than 15 miles per hour.

As our journey continued, she felt more comfortable and she started talking to us. The more relaxed she felt, the more we could see the relief come over her. As her fears subsided and she got to spend time with her children, my mother became a different woman. She was happier, stronger, better.

Things were going wonderfully for my family and soon my father ended up in a halfway house. He would call me, my siblings, and my mama, talking about how well he was doing. And as much as we all wanted to believe him, we knew he was manipulating us. Or at least *I* knew he was.

My father would call me, telling me stories about how everyone at the halfway house loved him and how they all called him The Godfather. He would talk about how great he was doing and then there would be a moment of silence. And every time that silence came, I knew what his next question was going to be. "So, Shane, are you going to drop the charges so I can get out?"

With that simple little sentence, my father ruined his chances of me wanting to let him out every time. He was a master manipulator, but I could read him like a book and his act didn't fool me at all.

My brother Ryan and my sister Kristy started to feel guilty and they wanted me to drop the charges so my dad could get out. They kept saying things like "I can really see the difference in him, Shane. He's doing great in the halfway house and I think he'll be even better if he can go home."

My older brother Keith and I had pretty much the same thoughts on the subject. Our father was an evil, vindictive bastard and we knew he was just trying to play all of us. We wanted him to stay as far away as possible because as far as we were concerned, he just couldn't be far away enough.

I knew my father had a terrible childhood and that now he had a chance to recover from all of his mental issues. His doctors said that he was psychotic, and maybe with more time, he would be able to get better. More than anything I wanted him to get better so we could have a real family for the first time in our lives.

But as time went on and the rest of the family kept begging, I felt like I had no choice but to let my father out. Ryan and Kristy didn't really understand how he was. They were never in a position where they had to financially support him for thirty-something years and they were never in a position where he tried to ruin their families. Since all of our experiences with my father were unique, we couldn't agree on the best thing to do with him.

I finally gave in and dropped the charges against my father. Not because I wanted to and not because I had to, but because I wanted to make the rest of my family happy. Ryan and Kristy were thrilled that their daddy was released and they couldn't thank me enough. Even my mother was happy to see him get out, but she was a little too happy in my opinion.

With all he had done to her for all those years and with all she saw him do to the rest of us, she still welcomed him back with open arms. So he moved into the trailer with her, and of course, transformed her once peaceful home into another living hell.

I resented my mother for taking him back and I still do. It's her life, though, and I can't help it if she wants to live with that demon. I'm not professing to be any kind of a saint, but I just wish my mother could have seen my father for who – and what – he truly was.

But with her eyes and thoughts blinded by love, my mother let herself get thrown into the ultimate fight between good and evil. She had to choose whether she was going to be with my father or if she was going to be with the rest of us. And since my dad was still there with her, it looked like evil won that battle.

Chapter 28

Orson Welles once said, "We're born alone, we live alone, we die alone. Only through our love and friendship can we create the illusion for the moment that we're not alone." His words are brilliant, but he's preaching to the choir.

I spent a long time living under the illusion of not being alone. I knew I didn't have much to do with my parents and my siblings, but I had other family and friends that made me feel like I was never alone. Between Kelli, the kids, and my friends, I thought I had it all. But once all of them were taken out of the picture, I didn't know much except that Orson Welles made one of the truest statements ever to be spoken.

After the Churchill Downs incident, I spent two and a half horrible months alone. I called almost everyone I knew to see if they could help me get reinstated and nobody knew how. I wanted to keep spending time with my family, but I couldn't now that my father was back around. That was the hardest two and a half months of my life and I didn't know how I would survive by myself.

Then one day I got an unexpected phone call from my friend Jerry Lasala at Arlington Park. When I picked up the phone, I was surprised to hear Jerry's chipper voice. I could almost hear his smile when he said, "Why don't you come here, man? Get outta there and come visit me."

"Jerry," I said, "You *know* I can't go anywhere near a Churchill Downs-owned racetrack," reminding him that Churchill and Arlington shared a common ownership, so I was barred from both. "What part of that don't you understand?"

Jerry replied, "You mean you can't come to Arlington Park?"

Still pissed off at the world and growing angrier by the second, I responded, "No, Jerry, but why don't you know that? You're a Guild representative. Why don't you know that?"

Jerry responded with the simple word, "Bullshit," and said he was going to call me back in a little while.

A little while later, my phone rang again. This time when I answered, I wasn't nearly as mad at Jerry's happy attitude. He said to me, "Shane, get on a plane because we have a meeting here in Chicago tomorrow morning at 10:00 a.m."

That was all I needed to hear. I packed up my things and made sure to put some pictures of Kelli and the kids in my suitcase. We may not have been together anymore, but that didn't mean I loved my family any less.

The next day when I arrived at Arlington Park, I went to Mr. Duchossois' office and sat next to Jerry at a big, long table. Dick Duchossois is not only the head of Arlington Park, but he also happens to be the largest shareholder in Churchill Downs, Inc. When the meeting started, Mr. Duchossois said, "Hey Shawn. I just wanna tell you that you're in. You're reinstated. It's done. All you have to do is get back on a plane, go in front of Steve Sexton and talk to him. Then it's over."

I was so happy to hear that news that I didn't even bother to tell him that my name wasn't Shawn. For some reason or another, he had always called me Shawn, so there was no need to correct him now. And since he was the one to get me reinstated, I was more than happy to let him call me whatever he wanted.

After that meeting, Jerry flew back with me to Louisville to help me verify my reinstatement. We met with Steve Sexton, the president of Churchill Downs, and things went wonderfully. We discussed everything that had happened and there were apologies all around. Then Steve told me I could officially start riding again on a certain date that was rapidly approaching. I thanked Steve over and over, thrilled that the problem was finally resolved.

I felt like a piece of my soul had been revived. I had felt empty for so long it almost felt strange to have a moment of happiness. I was thrilled that I could get back to my career and ride again – but with no one to share that happiness with, my excitement was short lived.

So much of my time was spent trying to figure out how I could be reinstated that it had become my sole ambition. But once I had the chance to ride again, I realized that I just didn't want to. After everything I had been through over the last couple of months, how could I act as if nothing ever happened and pick up where I left off?

The answer was that I couldn't. I couldn't bear the idea of sitting in the hot box again and joking around with the other jockeys. I was too hurt to do that. I spent half my life thinking that I had a family of friends and all of that was taken away from me. I was a one-man family now and I didn't see any way to change that.

I wanted my family back. Not just Kelli and my kids, but also my friends. I missed the comfort of always having company; of always feeling loved. All of that was taken away from me. I couldn't stand the idea of being around my friends because I felt they all betrayed me. I know someone could have stood up for me, but until Jerry Lasala stepped forward, nobody did anything.

So I stayed away from most of the riders I had been friends with and I chose to have nothing to do with them. Sure I felt lonely, but that was better than feeling brokenhearted all over again.

The only time I ever came out of my shell and went to see a rider was when Jerry Bailey retired. Jerry made me the rider that I was. Riding with him on an everyday basis on the best horses made me feel like a better man. That's just how Jerry was. It was almost impossible to spend time with him and not feel some of his goodness rub off on you.

While I was on my way to his retirement party, I kept reminding myself of all the reasons I wanted to be there. This was for Jerry, not for anyone else. Our sons were best friends and at one point, we were best friends, too. I had absolutely no qualms with Jerry and I wanted to be there for his big day. Though I definitely wasn't excited to see the rest of the jockeys, I genuinely wanted to be there for Jerry just like he was always there for me.

When I walked into the party, Jerry saw me and gave me a big hug. He looked as surprised as he looked happy when he said, "Shane! What are you doing?!"

I returned his hug and said, "Jerry, I don't want to be in this jocks' room, but I have all the respect for you in the world. You are a big part of why I turned out to be the rider I was. I admire you and I want to see you ride your last race."

Jerry patted me on the shoulder and said, "I love you." And even though I had been burned by a lot of people, I knew he meant it.

I told him I loved him too and then I prepared to leave. I had needed to see Jerry so I could congratulate him and wish him luck, but I didn't want to interfere with his big day. That day was supposed to be a happy one and I knew if I stayed there with the other riders, there were going to be a lot of unhappy faces.

As I was walking out, Mark Guidry walked up to me and said, "Hey lil' brother!"

I felt my body tense and my teeth clench when I heard his voice. Trying to keep my cool, I said, "Mark, I have nothing to say to you except that I wish you luck."

Then my brain wheels started turning and I said, "Wait. I do have something to say. You're my little boy's godfather and I'm not gonna say a bad word about you to my little boy. Just because me and you don't get along, just because we have our differences, I won't let it interfere with family."

Mark looked at me and I could feel my blood start to boil again while I continued talking to him. I brought up all the things I had done for him in the past; things I will never repeat because I made a promise to my close friend all those years ago. But he knew what I was talking about and he knew how serious I was.

Even though Mark wasn't solely responsible for me being ruled off, I felt more hurt – more betrayed – by him than by anybody. We were best friends. Brothers. And the fact that he didn't stand up for me showed me how little he really cared. If the situations were reversed, I would have never gone on and continued my career without him. I would have sat in the jocks' room until someone let him back. But when it came to me, Mark let me go without a fight.

Since I was too tired, too drained, and too devastated to fight with or for anybody anymore, I just left. I walked away from the situation and I left my old life behind me. As far as I was concerned, Shane Sellers was dead – killed by the people he loved the most.

And even though I was still very much alive, I couldn't have felt deader inside. The illusion was gone and I knew I was alone.

Part 5

The Long Road
To Coteau

Chapter 29

People love to read a good rags-to-riches story. It's always nice to see that someone overcame the odds, faced their adversaries, and paved their way to a better future. But that's not how my story went. I went from rags to riches back to rags.

Even though I made millions of dollars through the course of my career, I didn't have any liquid assets to show for it. My money was tied up in property, loans to friends, and the lifestyle I started living when I could afford the finer things in life. Now I couldn't afford the basic necessities in life, let alone the finer things. So all the money I made was for nothing. I was cash poor and I knew it.

I tried approaching some of the people I loaned money to over the years and hardly anybody was willing to give me a dime. My little girl's godfather owed me $7,500 from 15 years ago. I got him on the phone and said, "Listen: I wrote it off when I was making money, but now I need the money, man." He gave me $1,000 on three separate occasions. I called another guy who I loaned $3,000 and he wouldn't pay me anything.

When things got bad enough, I knew I was going to have to go through the money I had saved for my retirement. I had to tell Kelli about my decision and that was a hard conversation. I said, "Listen, I either use it now or when I'm 65. With everything I did to my body, I probably won't be in any condition to use it when I'm old – if I even make it to 65."

Kelli obviously didn't want to hear me talk about how I might not even make it to the age of retirement, but in the end she agreed that we would have to use that money. And even though I accepted the situation, I wasn't happy about it. I couldn't believe that I had given so many people so much money through all the years and nobody wanted to pay me back when I desperately needed the money. Instead, I watched my supposed friends parade around on new Harleys or driving sports cars, showing off all the assets I helped them get.

How ironic. Everything I ever stood for was for a group of riders. I wanted to make their lives better and I sacrificed my own life to do it. The first time I made a decision for me and my family, I lost everything. A decision for me and my family, not for anybody else. I didn't ask anyone. I just stood up for myself so I wouldn't lose my kids' futures. And because of that decision, all of us were left with nothing. And as my quest to regain some of the money I gave throughout the years showed, we were also left with nobody.

Out of sheer desperation, I approached Mike Smith, Pat Day, and trainer Billy Mott for help. We all owned a piece of property together and I wanted them to buy me out. To be more accurate, I *needed* them to buy me out. They knew I was cash poor, but still they didn't want to help me. Finally, out of either pity or guilt, or maybe both, they bought me out for one million dollars. Then they never spoke to me again.

So there I was with a million dollars and no idea of what to do with it. I knew that was a lot of money, but I also knew it wouldn't be enough for me to support myself and my family forever. We had around $10,000 a month in bills and those were just for the necessities. I always promised myself that my kids would have the finest of everything. How could I keep that promise if I didn't make more money?

As my sanity continued to wither away and I headed straight down the road to complete isolation, I tried to figure out my best options. I had one million dollars to invest in my kids' futures. Should I start my own business? Should I play the stocks? Should I put it all in a high interest bank account? What should I do?

The more I thought about my options, the more hopeless I felt. I didn't know anything about running a business, nor did I know anything about finances. Hell, the first two years I rode I didn't pay Uncle Sam because I didn't even know that income tax existed. How could I hope to be a banking wizard now?

It didn't take me long to realize that there was only one thing I knew. I knew the horse racing industry. And even though I couldn't and wouldn't ride anymore, I knew there had to be some other way for me to stick with what I knew best.

When I was on vacation in Louisiana, Kenny Desormeaux asked me to go with him to check out a farm in Coteau, just a short distance away from Erath. I always wanted to break babies and to be the kind of horse owner that jockeys would be happy to work with; to be an owner like Barry Golden. So the idea of investing my money in a farm lifted my spirits right up.

The property was big. It was huge. I had seen the place before and I knew it had a reputation. That was where big gambling parties took place and the high rollers used the many bedrooms for late-night fun with local prostitutes. Though I never visited the place at that time, I knew all about it. Everyone in the area did. But even with its bad reputation, the property seemed perfect.

As I walked around the place, I saw all of its potential. With a total of 26 acres, I had more than enough room to do anything I wanted. The front was five acres and I could board horses there. The walking wheel was already in place. I had 20 stalls for horses. On the left side of the barn was a kitchen that opened up into a big sun room. I even had a house and an apartment upstairs. The yard was so spacious that I could play a game of hide and seek and never find who I was looking for.

All in all, the property was just what I needed. It was going to need a bit of work, but that was fine by me. So without thinking twice, I paid $500,000 cash and secured myself a beautiful piece of property where I could grow old. I just wished that the rest of my family was there to grow old with me.

But alas, my family was gone. I still talked on the phone with Kelli all the time, but we had too many problems. She knew I wasn't the man she married and she saw how quickly I was falling apart. The last thing she wanted to do was to tear our kids out of their schools and away from their friends in Kentucky to go live in Louisiana with a man who was quickly losing his mind.

Looking back, I can't blame Kelli for her decision. I *wasn't* the man I used to be and I knew it. Every day became such a battle for me that I could hardly stand the thought of getting out of bed. There I was with an enormous farm and I didn't know what to do with it. I had spent half a million dollars to buy it and another couple hundred thousand dollars to remodel it. But even with my new posh living room, my beautiful home, and my gorgeous trophy room, I still felt empty inside.

I was so depressed that I didn't want to see or talk to anybody. I just wanted to be alone because that's how I felt: alone. As the days turned to weeks and the lawn turned into a jungle, I continued to lie there in my own misery.

Finally one day I decided that I had enough and I had to get up. As miserable as I was, I knew I needed to get out into the world and try to start living again. Kelli was gone and that was a cold, hard fact. So I ignored my hurt feelings and I started looking around for someone to fill the void in my heart. I knew I could never replace Kelli, but I would feel at least a little better if I wasn't completely alone.

I started going out to bars again and I found a lot more liquor than I did women. Every night I went out drinking, washing down pain pills with shot after shot of liquor. I was heading down a really bad path, but at that time, I hardly cared.

While I was in a drunken stupor, I tried to find someone to help ease my loneliness. I met a woman who wanted to be with me – or at least I thought she wanted to be with me. Ignoring my logic,

I just accepted her willingness as a sign of affection. If this woman wanted me, then there had to be a good reason for it.

As it turned out, there was a good reason and it had nothing to do with feelings. This woman was young – only 24-years-old – and she loved horses almost as much as I did. She always agreed with everything I said, even when she knew I was wrong. At the time, that's what I thought I needed, so our relationship moved forward at a very rapid pace. Within a couple of months, she was living with me at my farm and she was officially my girlfriend.

She took care of me the way I thought I needed to be taken care of. I didn't know much about banking, so she took care of all the bills. I didn't know much about being on the verge of a divorce, so she showed me how to handle that situation, too. She did a lot of things that I thought were helpful at the time.

Then the illusion slowly disappeared again and I could finally see the reality.

Kelli didn't have a problem with the fact that I was dating another woman, or even that I was living with one. But when Kelli started getting phone calls from this woman's ex-boyfriend, she had a BIG problem. At first, his phone calls were anonymous. He would tell Kelli that she'd better be careful because his ex was nothing more than a common thief. As he kept calling, he revealed more information and told Kelli he knew all about my girlfriend's thievery because she stole everything from him.

When Kelli told me that, I refused to listen. I thought she was just acting jealous or that maybe she was losing her mind, too.

This was my girlfriend. She lived with me. Surely I would know if she was stealing from under my nose. That was the stance I took and I held firm to my beliefs for a good, long while.

Then I started getting phone calls from Kelli saying that she was receiving shut-off notices from the electric company. I knew that was impossible because my girlfriend paid all the bills. Still, I asked her and she said, "I already told you I paid that bill. Kelli's just trying to cause problems between us!"

Still enchanted by this woman like a sailor is to a Siren, I refused to believe Kelli. She already showed me what she thought of me when she drew the divorce papers. As far as I was concerned, Kelli was just trying to make me more miserable than I already was.

Unfortunately, what I assumed was Kelli's paranoia turned out to be my mental blindness. One day my girlfriend's mother called because she said that her daughter stole her old checkbook and wrote out checks with it. It was one thing to ignore your soon-to-be ex-wife's warnings, but it was another to ignore what your girlfriend's mother had to say. If she could sink so low as to do that to her own mother, what was she capable of doing to me?

As time quickly showed, she was capable of doing a lot. Kelli and the kids lost their electricity and I lost a whole lot more. When I started looking into the situation, things just didn't add up. My money was almost gone and I didn't know where it all went. Kelli's wedding ring disappeared. Even the gold Rolex I received as a gift from a sheik in Dubai was missing. Everything was gone — and as soon as I realized that, so was my girlfriend.

In the end, she went to jail, but she apparently didn't learn her lesson. To this day, police officers occasionally knock on my door asking if I know where she is. She has many warrants out on her because she also stole from a lot of other poor saps who fell for her like I did. She stole from a lot of people and she cost us all a lot of money.

But the most valuable thing she cost me was all the time I could have been spending with my real family.

Chapter 30

You know that saying, "Hell hath no fury like a woman scorned?" That's a good saying. I've seen some scorned women in my time and they aren't playing around. If we had armies filled with scorned women, nobody would dare wage a war against us. But what happens when a man is scorned? In my case, I was just in Hell.

After I lost almost all my money, I knew I was in serious trouble. At one point I had a million dollars and now I was concerned about my financial status. At that point, I would have been happy to have a million pennies because there was no cash left.

I spent months trying to borrow money from anyone I was still in contact with. One by one, everyone I knew turned me down. I couldn't even get a loan from the bank because I didn't have any income yet from the farm. I tried to explain that this loan was so I could *get* an income, but nobody wanted to hear it.

The only thing I had to fall back on was the best horse I ever owned. He was sired by a horse a used to ride; a stallion named Good & Tough. I won some great races on him, so I was able to breed one of my mares to him for free. When the time came, I brought the baby horse back to the farm and just looked at him, thinking, "What am I gonna name him?"

After a bit of thought, I said to myself, "You know what? They always called me Renegade. So I'm gonna call him SS

Renegade. Hopefully we'll all watch him run and people will say, 'There goes SS Renegade.' That's Shane Sellers' Renegade." Even though I never considered myself as a rebel, that name seemed perfect. My horse wasn't an outlaw, but he was all mine.

SS Renegade was one hell of a horse, too. I wanted him to be the next big racehorse to come from Louisiana. Even with all the time I spent living and traveling to places like Kentucky, Chicago, and Florida, I was still a Louisiana boy all the way. And just like my home state was noted for producing some of the best jockeys in the world, I wanted SS Renegade to be the first in a line of phenomenal Louisiana-bred horses.

That was my plan and that's how I trained him. I didn't want to be one of the many owners and trainers who make a horse work too hard or too fast. I didn't want to numb his legs by "blocking" the feeling in his nerves with a shot so he could run no matter how sore he might have felt. I didn't want to ever see him on the wrong side of a green tarp because he was just pushed too far. No, I didn't want any of that for my horse.

I wanted SS Renegade to shine. Not because he was drugged to do so and not because he was worked like a slave horse. I wanted him to shine naturally because that was in his character. This horse was going to be a winner and I knew it.

The great thing was that being around a horse that was a winner made *me* feel like a winner. Shortly after I got SS Renegade, my farm was finally ready for business. I was going to raise and train a lot of great horses and I couldn't wait.

On opening day, I threw a party at my farm to celebrate. My band came to play with me, a lot of my friends came, and my family came, too. In the time my father had been released, the family started talking again. Things were finally getting better. So when I planned my party, I called up my parents and said, "Mom and Dad, I'm having a party. If you want, you're welcome to come." And even though I never really got along with my father, I was very happy to see my parents at my party.

Everything was going wonderfully at the party and we were all having a lot of fun. Everyone was smiling and laughing, eating and dancing. I sang some songs with my band and then my father decided that he wanted to sing a couple of songs, too. Letting the happy mood of the party take me over, I told my dad to get right up there and sing his heart out. He sang one song. He sang two. And from the looks of it, he was going to stay up there and sing the night away. I was really glad to see him so happy, so I let him have his fun and sing until he couldn't sing anymore.

When my dad finished and my parents were just about ready to leave, I went to give him a hug. I was a little bit drunk, but I was a happy kind of drunk – or so I thought. With a smile on my face, I said to him, "Dad, I hope you're proud, man, because you know you were hard on us but we were respectful kids. We turned out to be respectful people and you see all these people here."

I pointed around to everyone who was wearing a green shirt with the S&S Farms logo and smiled some more. Still pointing to all the people who were there to help me, I said, "Ya know, all these people would be here for me in a heartbeat if I needed them." That was a feeling I hadn't experienced in a long time, so I was really glad to say it.

My dad wasn't nearly as happy for me as I was, though. For some reason, he thought I was looking to start a fight. He stepped into my personal space and put his face close to mine when he snarled, "They'd be here for you or for me?"

I looked at my father in shock and didn't say a word. Even though he stayed silent, I knew he was mad. I almost thought he was going to pull out a pair of boxing gloves for us to fight things out like when I was a kid.

But for me, those days were over. I was done having him treat me like garbage and I wasn't going to take it – especially not at my own party. With years of resentment and pain as my guide, I grabbed his arm from behind and pulled it up by his shirt. My teeth felt like fangs when I practically growled, "Get outta here. Get off my property. Get out right now!"

Never one to walk away from a potential fight, my father said, "No, no, no." Then he repeated his question. "They'd be here for you or for me?"

With an attitude as lethal as my father's, I responded, "Well, I guess they'd be here for me."

A wild look came over his eyes when he started shouting, "Well bring them on! Bring the motherfuckers on! I'll show them. I'll show all of them!"

Horrified by the way my father was acting at *my* party in front of *my* guests, I grabbed him and yelled, "Get off my property!"

I couldn't believe he was doing this to me. This was supposed to be my big day and just like every other big day of my life, my father was destroying it. All I wanted was to show him that I was accomplishing something; that I had become someone. And just like old times, all he wanted was to show me who was boss. Well, I wasn't going to let that happen. I had officially had enough and I wasn't going to take his shit ever again.

I wasn't a little boy anymore and I wasn't going to act like one. Leading my father to his car like a parent leads a child, I called him every name in the book. When I went to put him in the car and he brought his face closer to mine, I got right back up in his face. I said, "I dare you to pick your hand up. Come on, let's get it on. You wanna go? I weigh 150 pounds now. I'm not 112 anymore, so come on."

Surprisingly enough, my father didn't raise his hand. He didn't do much of anything. He just stood there listening while I cussed him out. Then he turned to my mother and said, "Hey, you better tell him to shut his mouth."

Still fuming, I turned his attention back to me and said, "No. Mama can't help you now, buddy. You're not as tough as you think you are. You're not as tough as you always made *us* think you are. You wanna whip me? Then come on!"

But after all those years and all those threats, he never made a move. He just got in the car with my mama and left the party. After that, our relationship pretty much ended. My mother was thrown into the middle of our fight and I couldn't see her. I lived right there in Louisiana, practically right down the street, and I couldn't go visit my mother. My brothers and sister took my father's side, too, so I couldn't see them, either. None of my family wanted anything to do with me anymore. That was that.

And to think, this all started over a party. Imagine what growing up in this family was like for all the occasions that *weren't* worth celebrating.

Chapter 31

They say blood is thicker than water. I don't know who *they* are, but they obviously didn't come from *my* family.

A few months after my father and I got into that fight at my party, I heard that he wasn't doing so well. My little brother was concerned, so I picked up the phone and prepared to talk to my father for the first time in months. When he answered the phone, I said, "Look, I apologize for what happened."

In his typical style, he responded, "Yeah, you better never do nothing like that again. Ya know, get up in my face." As he spoke, I could almost hear the hateful look I knew was on his face.

I said, "Look, I didn't call you for that, man. I called to apologize." My temper started to flare as I continued, "I just wanted to fucking apologize and you wanna talk about fighting like you're gonna whip my ass. Why didn't you raise your hand then? If you wanted to fight, then why didn't you raise your hand, you motherfucker?"

Of course that led to another fight and the two of us were ready to rip each other's throats out right through the phone. As always, he didn't think he did anything wrong because he could only see things from his point of view.

When he finally calmed down, I sucked up my pride and went to my parents' trailer to talk to him. He was sitting in that wooden chair with the most depressed face I had ever seen. It hurt me to see him that way. In the back of my mind I wondered why I always cared so much about what he thought or about how he felt, since he clearly didn't care about my feelings.

Pushing those thoughts aside, I got down on my knee and hugged him, telling him how much I loved him. Then I told him I might go back to riding and that I would love to have him come to the farm to help me train. He worked me to the bone when I was a kid, but his training methods were successful. Whether he had me hit the punching bag, or run, or box, he always knew how to get me into great shape. So I figured that maybe we could do the same thing again now to lift both our spirits.

My mama was thrilled by my suggestion and so was my brother Ryan. Both of them got really excited and it was all they could talk about. They waited for me to call my dad to tell him to come over, but every time I picked up the phone to call, I felt absolutely sick. I wanted to stay true to my word, but I couldn't bring myself to call him.

All those years of hurt finally caught up to me and I didn't have it in me to look out for my dad when I couldn't even look out for myself. As hard as I tried, I just couldn't bring myself to talk to him. I take partial responsibility for that fact, but it wasn't all my fault. I always wanted to be a good son and I wanted him to be proud of me. And even though I know he loved me, it hurt that he could never show it.

So I didn't call my father and I still haven't talked to him to this day. Since he and my mama come as a group package, that means I can't see her, either. I know he scared her for all those years, but that wasn't my choice. I had him put away so my mama could live a better life. Even after all her crying while we rode through the swamp in that little boat, she still ran back to him when he got out. She chose him over me; over the whole family. It hurt to know that I lived right down the road and I couldn't visit them, but that was their decision, not mine. They lost out on a pretty terrific son and I hoped they knew that. But they were both sick, him being crazy and her being brainwashed, so there was really nothing I could do but mentally say goodbye to both of them.

I tried to fill the emptiness in my life by spending all of my time with my prized horse. He was the first young horse on my new farm, and I spent a lot of time breaking him. In a way, SS Renegade became like a substitute for the rest of my family. Since I couldn't be with anyone else in my family, I devoted all of my time and attention to him.

Of course, I still talked to Kelli and the kids, and I talked to them frequently. Kelli and I would sit on the phone together, talking about how much we loved each other. Then we would try to talk through our problems and we would both end up crying. We wanted to be together, but at that time, our relationship seemed like an impossibility.

Kelli and the kids were still in Kentucky and that's where their lives were based. My kids had friends there, they went to school there, and they were comfortable there. They didn't have to move around in a mobile home while we traveled from state to state, following the races anymore. They had a steady home and they loved it.

So every time Kelli and I brought up the idea of getting back together, I knew how the conversation was going to end. Like every other time, we would hang up the phone with more hurt feelings and two more puddles of tears.

I'm not ashamed to say that I cried over the loss of my family because I know that doesn't make me less of a man. My family was all I had – it's *still* all I have. Every tear I shed was like a wet droplet of love and remorse flowing out of my body. I wanted to be with them; to see my kids grow up. I just didn't know how to make the situation work.

As I fell deeper and deeper into depression, I tried to pretend that everything was all right by bonding with my horse. SS Renegade got me through a lot, but there was one thing he couldn't help me with: my finances. All of the cash was gone and I couldn't support myself anymore, let alone my family. Nobody would loan me any money, though, so I had to do whatever it took to make sure we could all survive.

I had a new tractor that was worth $20,000 and I sold it for $10,000 just so I could get through another month of bills. While that money quickly flowed out, I tried to find anything else I could sell; anything that was expendable. The problem was I didn't have anything that I could get rid of and make money off it. For the life of me, I couldn't figure out what else to sell, so I continued to grow more miserable while I waited for an opportunity to present itself.

Then came the day when Kelli called me to say the water was turned off. I couldn't believe what she was telling me. I promised my kids everything in the world and now I couldn't even provide them with a good bath? If I didn't love my family so much, I think I would have killed myself to end the pain and the struggle. But I loved my family way too much to do that, so I had to come up with a fast solution.

Unfortunately, the only solution to my family's problems was who I considered to be a member of the family: SS Renegade. He was a great horse and according to Steve Asmussen, the number one trainer in the country, and my calculations, he was worth about $40,000. I didn't want to sell him, but I had no choice. It was either sell my horse or let my kids go dirty and starving. So even though I loved SS Renegade more than I ever loved any other animal, I had to do what was best for my human family. I had to give him a kiss on his nose and say goodbye.

One of the few friends I had left offered to buy SS Renegade. He told me he would buy SS Renegade for $15,000. When I heard that figure, my heart broke. This horse was like family to me and I didn't want to let him go. Still, $15,000 was his final offer and I had to take it.

When SS Renegade left, it felt like the rest of my soul left with him. I had to sell a piece of myself – the only real friend I had left – for a little less than a third of what he was worth. If I planned to sell him in the future, things might have been different. But that was never my intention. I had wanted SS Renegade to be the first horse I ever bred and to be a real runner. I wanted to fill up my farm with him and his family as much as I wanted to fill it with me and my family. I had a lot of great plans for SS Renegade and I felt lost without him.

Now the only hope I had was that I trained SS Renegade well enough that I could at least be his fan. I could go to his races and watch his mane fly in the wind while he galloped towards victory. And that might not have seemed like much, but it was the only hope I had left in me.

A few months later, that opportunity finally arose. I was mindlessly walking around a store when I ran into a man I knew from Evangeline Downs. He greeted me with a smile and said, "Hey Shane! How've you been?"

Since I couldn't answer that question honestly without startling him, I said, "I'm doing just fine. How are you?"

When I heard what he had to say next, I was better than fine. I was on top of the world. He told me that Evangeline Downs was going to host the Cajun Jockey Challenge where a number of retired and active jockeys would be honored. And even with all I had been through, he wanted me to be one of the guests of honor.

I couldn't believe my luck. It seemed that my world was finally changing. Evangeline Downs wanted to honor me at one of their biggest events. Better yet, SS Renegade was going to run his first race that day. Against all odds, I was going to be honored with my favorite horse right there with me.

Without asking for any more details, I accepted the informal invitation and confirmed that nothing in the world would keep me away. From what I was told, I was the first jockey to commit to the occasion. I was so excited that I planned to be the first jockey to walk onto the track on the day of the event.

When I got home that day, I was happier than I had been in years. I began my career at Evangeline Downs and I knew a lot of other Cajun jockeys who did the same. Those men were mentors to me as much as I was a mentor to several of them. I was really nervous to see some of those men again, but I was looking forward to getting back into the racing world and getting back on the industry's good side. This was exactly what I needed to get out of my slump and feel like a real person again.

In the months that led up to the Cajun Jockey Challenge, I ran down to my mailbox everyday to see if my invitation had arrived yet. When it wasn't there, I would go back upstairs, crack open a beer, and lie on the couch, eagerly awaiting the mailman's next delivery. I didn't know exactly when the Challenge was, but I knew my invitation had to arrive very soon.

As days turned into weeks, it started to look like someone forgot me; that my invitation was either lost or not coming. Starting to get nervous, I called Evangeline Downs three different times to ask about my invitation and the Challenge in general. Every time I called, I was told, "Your invitation was sent out and you will get it shortly."

Each person I spoke to told me I was going to play an important role at the event. As time proved, I was only allowed to play the role of the scapegoat. My invitation never arrived and the Challenge went on without me.

The day of the Cajun Jockey Challenge, I was washing some horses and listening to my radio, wondering when on earth I would get my invitation. That's when an announcement on the radio stated that I, Shane Sellers, was going to be at the event in just a few hours. I couldn't believe my ears. I was so shocked that I had to sit down on a soapy, wet chair. Every person I spoke to lied to me about my invitation, but they still had the nerve to broadcast the fact that I was supposed to be there?

Outraged, I picked up the phone and called Evangeline Downs for a fourth time. I spoke to a woman named Christine who was incredibly embarrassed about the situation. She said, "I'm so sorry Mr. Sellers! Do you think you'll be able to make it?"

I replied, "No, I can't make it! The races are in a few hours and I can't find anyone else to mind the farm. Even if I could, how am I supposed to fill up a table of six at the last second?"

Now feeling as angry as I was hurt, I told Christine, "Please, whatever you do, just don't let my fans think I wasn't there because I didn't want to be."

Christine assured me that everyone would know how much I wanted to be there, and then we hung up. But my fans never got to hear my side of the story. Instead, they heard almost the exact opposite.

The lies didn't end there, either. I read an article where Jason Boulet, the Racing Secretary of Evangeline Downs, stated, "All of these athletes have strong ties to this area; even though many no longer compete here on a regular basis, this is and always will be home to them."

This was all news to me. I wanted nothing more than to attend the Cajun Jockey Challenge, pay tribute to Louisiana racing, and see SS Renegade run his first race. Unfortunately, Evangeline Downs made it perfectly clear that I was not welcome at my supposed home, despite the fact that they promoted my alleged confirmation until the day of the event.

When I listened to that radio announcement and then read that article, I felt the small piece that was left of my heart shatter into a million black pieces. The first time I heard about the Challenge, I felt like I was on top of the world. Now that Evangeline Downs let the Challenge go on without even inviting me, I felt like I was back in Hell again.

Out of everything that ever happened to me in the racing world, that may have been the most heartbreaking moment for me. I was devastated. Every time I thought of the empty seat bearing my name on it, I felt as crushed as I felt when I was first shunned from Churchill Downs. It killed me to know that TVG announced that I missed my flight to Louisiana and that so many other people thought I wasn't interested enough to attend.

But the truth was that I had always been interested in the horse racing industry; it just wasn't interested in *me*.

When I had that realization, I decided that something had to be done. I couldn't keep sitting back and letting any of my remaining fans think that I didn't care. I had made my voice heard on many other occasions and I was going to do the same now.

But this time I wasn't going to take my problems to the TV circuit or the newspapers. I wanted more than a quarter page article that described my current predicament. The truth needed to be told and it needed to be told in full. People needed to know why I disappeared in the first place and why it looked like I was still missing.

The public might not have known it, but I never went anywhere. I was sitting here the whole time, just wishing that people could understand what had happened better than I could understand it myself.

And when I met a young woman named Tricia Psarreas, I knew that the only way to make my whole story heard was to put it all in a book.

Chapter 32

Whenever things go wrong in life, people say things like, "Don't worry. God has a plan." While the idea of God planning out our lives is comforting, it would be nice if he clued us in to what his plan actually is.

Even with everything I've gone through in my life, I still believe that God has a plan for all of us. Sometimes that plan isn't what we expect and sometimes we can't understand where His plan is heading. But God has a plan and when He's ready to share it, everything will fall into place.

For years I couldn't figure out why God planned for me to lose everything, but once I met Trish, I saw that maybe I was part of something bigger than I originally thought. Maybe my life story wasn't just about me; maybe it was about something greater than I — or any other individual — could ever be.

When Trish and I first met to start putting this book together, the situation was awkward at best. She and her friend Sheryl Maloney flew to Louisiana and stayed at my farm for a few days over the summer. They followed me around with video cameras and notebooks, trying to grasp everything that had ever happened to me in just a few short days.

At first I felt uncomfortable sharing my home with two complete strangers. Everywhere I went, they went. If I was lying on my couch watching TV, they were there. If I was cleaning the stables, they were there, too. No matter where I went, those two managed to find me and talk more about every bad thing that ever happened in my life.

The more I told them about my story, the more interested they became. They had a lot of questions to ask and I was irritated that they kept interrupting my stories to find out more. I was in a really bad frame of mind and it took a while before I got used to all their questions.

Even though Trish was upfront with me when she told me that she knew next to nothing about horse racing, I was amazed to see how truthful she was about that fact. And even though it bothered me that I had to explain every little thing about horse racing, I grew to find Trish and Sheryl more interesting as time went on.

When I asked Trish what exactly she did know about horses, she responded, "My great-grandfather was a huge horse racing fan and spent a lot of time at Suffolk Downs. Once he flew down to see the Florida Derby and I think that was one of the highlights of his life."

She thought a bit more and continued, "Oh, I have a pony in Greece that looks like a dog with a horse's head, too." She then proceeded to show me a picture and I couldn't help but laugh. Her pony really was the size of a dog with a thoroughbred-sized head on it.

Trish then continued, "To be perfectly honest, Shane, I love horses but I've never even been to a horse race."

Sheryl chimed in, "Yes you have. Don't forget about *Wheel of Fortune!*"

Trish nodded her head quickly and said, "Oh, you're right! I did see one horse race." Then she grumbled something about the unfairness of *Wheel of Fortune.*

What I gathered from that conversation was that Trish and Sheryl went to Suffolk Downs to audition for *Wheel of Fortune.* Based on their bitterness towards the show at that moment, it appeared that neither of them made it. But at least my co-writer made it to Suffolk Downs for some reason and she had one horse racing experience under her belt.

As the weekend went on, the awkwardness faded away. Trish and Sheryl both had the gift of gab and it was hard to feel uncomfortable around them. So once that weird phase passed, I took them out to see some of Louisiana and what it had to offer. I knew we weren't doing anything all that grand, but I'll never forget their looks of excitement as they took their first bites of alligator or when I brought them to a Southern karaoke bar. The sight of real cowboys with hats and chaps was almost too much for them and I couldn't help but laugh at how amazing everything seemed to them.

From that point on, their time in Louisiana flew right by. We went out for food and drinks, had a barbeque, and sat down for interviews whenever we could. I even showed them my old house in Erath and all the damage Hurricane Katrina caused in the area. They were shocked to see the FIMA trucks and the half-empty cemeteries that were left in the wake of the damage. When they saw these things, they didn't even have to ask any questions because by that point I knew them well enough to answer their potential questions ahead of time.

But even though I knew they were interested in my story and they wanted to learn as much as they could, it got to be too much. One night I couldn't even get out of my bed because I was having such a bad anxiety attack. After my Xanax started working, I rejoined Trish and Sheryl, but I didn't have it in me to talk about my life any more than we already had.

Soon after, the girls packed up their notes and tapes and headed off to the airport. It was time for them to return to Massachusetts and time for the real work to begin.

After they left, I settled back into my empty home and called Kelli to tell her about our weekend. She was really happy for me and glad to see that I was going to do something for myself. I told her that Trish really thought this book would help me put my past behind me and I agreed. Kelli said, "I really hope so, baby," and I knew she meant it.

It took us a long time to get there, but Kelli and I were finally trying to repair our relationship. She and the kids would come down to Louisiana for a week or two and spend time with me. I was so happy to be around my family again that every moment we spent together felt magical. But soon they would leave again and I would feel more alone than I had ever felt before.

Then during one of their trips, something amazing happened. Kelli and I had a serious talk and decided we wanted to work things out. We both knew we loved each other and we both wanted our family to be together. Now we were finally ready to make the changes we needed to make for our relationship to work.

Kelli sat me down and held onto my hands. She looked me in the eye and asked, "What do you want, baby? Do you want to live this life or do you want to be with your family?"

I looked back into Kelli's eyes and spoke with all the sincerity I had when I replied, "I want my family. I want you. I want the kids. I want it all."

Kelli's voice shook a little when she said, "If you want to party and play with different chicks, that's your choice. But if you want to be a good father and husband and be with us, then you're going to be the best that you can be."

I looked at Kelli and marveled at the woman she had become. She wasn't a needy young girl anymore; she was all woman. And when I took Kelli into my arms at that moment, I knew she was all the woman I would need for the rest of my life.

Chapter 33

Woodrow Wilson once said, "I would never read a book if it were possible for me to talk half an hour with the man who wrote it." What a fantastic quote. One sentence shouts so many truths, but what happens when nobody wants to speak with the man behind the book?

That was the problem I encountered when Trish and I started working together. I wanted to share my story, but I needed some help to do so. Trish already knew everything about me from my perspective, but she needed to hear it from some other people, too. More importantly, *I* needed to hear it. I had so many questions that were never answered that I just wanted someone – anyone – to explain why I deserved so many of the things I went through.

I started calling people who might be able to help me; who might be able to make me feel sane again. But the more times I picked up the phone, the less I understood. I wanted to know why I was banned from Churchill Downs and why the industry forgot about me. Nobody could answer those questions, though, and there didn't seem to be an answer in sight.

The first person I called was Jerry Bailey and I expected our conversation to go perfectly. Unfortunately, things didn't quite go the way I planned. Until that moment, I never had a confrontation with Jerry. But on that particular day at that particular time, I couldn't accept the fact that he didn't know how to answer my questions. The longer we spoke, the more I felt everything from my past hit me. I started shouting and crying, just trying to make him understand. The last words he said to me before he hung up the phone were, "You got fucked, Shane. You got fucked. What do you want me to do?"

When we got off the phone, I was shocked. This was Jerry Bailey and that's what he had to say to me? "You got fucked?" That was something I already knew, but hearing it from him struck a nerve and made me feel like I was getting fucked all over again.

Soon after I got off the phone with Jerry, I made the mistake of calling Gary Stevens. I was still in a horrid mood and I cried the whole time we spoke. Gary didn't have any answers for me, either, and that made me feel even more horrible inside.

Most of the phone calls I made were unsuccessful, but I didn't really fall apart until I got in touch with Darrell Haire from the Jockey's Guild. When I had called him from the jocks' room at Churchill Downs, he told me that we would take the racetrack to court if I got handcuffed. It took me two years to get in contact with him again after that, and when I did, he insisted that he never said such a thing. I may have been in the middle of a mental breakdown, but I still knew an outright lie when I heard one. And since I can still vividly remember our conversation from three years ago, I knew Darrell was flat-out lying.

I called Trish to tell her what happened and she started making phone calls, too. Some people wouldn't take her call, others would simply hang up on her, and others went so far as to have their lawyers contact her. Trish was getting nowhere as quickly as I was, but at least she didn't know the people who made her feel less human.

Not only was it hard for Trish to find people to take her calls, but it was also hard for her to find people to take her money. She contacted The Permanently Disabled Jockey Fund twice before she got a return phone call. When she finally did get a call back from a woman named Nancy, Trish thought our luck might be changing. But Nancy said she would have to find out whether or not it was okay for us to donate a portion of the proceeds from our book to her organization. Since Nancy never called back, it became clear that our money was just as unwelcome as we were.

Imagine that. A charitable organization that has the potential to help hundreds of jockeys wouldn't even let us contribute to their supposed cause.

In the midst of all these phone calls, Kelli and the kids moved back home with me in Louisiana. I was thrilled to have them back, but I was not acting like the kind of man I wanted my family to see. Despite the happiness I felt with my family, I was not a happy man. One minute I would be screaming and the next minute I would be crying. Sometimes I screamed and cried at the same time. It was like someone else had taken over my mind and I could no longer control my brain or my body. I didn't know who I was, but I sure wasn't Shane anymore.

Still acting like someone else had taken over my body, I went on two separate trips to Boston to meet with Trish. Both of the trips had their fair share of ups and downs, and Trish could finally see what I described to her over the phone. She barely even knew me and she could tell this wasn't the same Shane she met over the summer.

When I went to Boston for the first time, I tried to keep my feelings under control. Trish and Sheryl picked me up at the airport and took me to a restaurant called Kowloon where they promised me the best Chinese food I would ever eat. They were right about the delicious food and I tried to keep my mind focused on the dishes and bowls and platters that covered our table. When I couldn't eat anymore and I could feel my anger returning, I decided to focus on what the girls described as the best Scorpion Bowls in the world. Before then I had never heard of a Scorpion Bowl. But when I saw the jumbo bowl filled with various types of liquor and three foot long straws, I agreed that there could be nothing better. After we finished two Scorpion Bowls and a couple other drinks, the girls took me to a local bar where I continued to drink my worries away.

All the while, I wore a smile that never reached my heart.

The next day we sat down to do some work and my temper was on the rise. Kelli and I had been angrily text messaging each other back and forth all night and I was afraid she wouldn't be there when I got home. This time when I tried to fake a smile, it didn't work quite as well.

I acted as polite as I could when I met Tricia's mother Anna and I felt comfortable enough around her to call her "Mom." I acted just as polite when some reporters from The Daily Item came to interview Trish and me. My politeness scale reached its max when I met Tricia's grandparents Van and Joanne, and later her aunt Mary and her uncle Mike. All of these people were very nice and they tried to make me feel right at home. However, as the day went on and my anger continued to flare, my smile slowly faded into a grimace.

By the end of the night, I couldn't even pretend to be happy or to be normal. I had dealt with so many people who claimed to have my best interest at heart that I couldn't take it anymore. All of the phone calls and confrontations got to me and something inside of me snapped. Unfortunately, my breakdown happened at Tricia's house in front of her, her mother, and Sheryl.

I was so angry and brokenhearted that I just started yelling and screaming, wearing circles into the wooden floor around the kitchen table. My anger wasn't directed at any of the women in my presence, but they were the ones who heard the brunt of it. Swears flew out of my mouth like they never had before and my voice rose to octaves I didn't know existed.

Anna and Trish tried to calm me down, but I was on a mental rampage. Things got so bad that Anna started yelling at me and I yelled right back at her. Trish jumped up from her chair to defend her mother and yelled, "Shane, take your shit and get the hell out of my house!"

I said, "Fine! You want me gone? I'll leave." Looking away from Trish, I pointed my gaze at Sheryl and asked, "Can you get me out of here and take me to my hotel? Just get me the hell out of here and get me back to my room."

Anna interjected, "No! Sheryl's like a daughter to me and you're not going anywhere with her when you're acting like that." Then she threw down a $20 bill and told me to take a cab back to my hotel.

At that point I was so mad I was shaking. I tried to gather up all my papers to put them in my briefcase and they fell all over the floor. I bent down, crinkling my papers and bending my pictures as I scooped them up, jamming them into my briefcase that didn't want to close. As I walked outside into the snow, I took a final look at Trish and shouted, "I offered you the world and you're walking away from the best thing that could have ever happened to you."

She came up to the door, her anger feeding off my fury, and said, "I don't give a damn," as she slammed the door in my face.

Unable to believe what had just happened, I stood outside in the freezing cold, gathering my jacket around myself. I didn't want to fight with anyone. That was never my intention. But the man I was becoming gradually came out to the point where these people that I considered family didn't even want me in their home.

While I stood outside waiting for my taxi, I threw my briefcase in the snow and ignored my soaking wet papers and pictures. As I walked away from my belongings, Trish stepped onto her porch wearing her fuzzy purple slippers and no jacket. She tried to get me to talk to her, but I had nothing to say. With my arms wrapped across my chest, I just said, "Your true colors came out, Trish. I've seen your true colors now."

Apparently, that pissed her off more than anything that had transpired that night. She responded, "My true colors? How dare you! All I want to do is help you and you're acting like a crazy person. I've listened to your stories and grown a passion for this book; for this cause. You think I want to walk away? Of course I don't. But if this is how you're going to act, how the hell am I supposed to work with you?"

I didn't want to talk to her anymore and I turned my back to the brick wall outside her house. Gripping onto the freezing wrought iron fence, I tried to ignore her and everything she was saying. As hard as I tried, she just wouldn't go away; she just wouldn't let me be.

The more I heard her voice telling me how much she cared about me and what a great friend I had become to her, the more my mind ate at me. I kept trying to push her away, but she kept on coming. She put her hands on my shoulders and tried to give me a hug. When I didn't respond, she wrapped her arms around me and whispered, "I love you, Shane, and I want to help you get through this. You're family now."

When I heard that, the floodgates broke open. I started crying; sobbing. I cried for everything I had been through and everything that had yet to come. I cried and cried until I fell to my knees in the snow. And Trish sat there the whole time, holding me and trying to comfort me with her soft words. We stayed in the snow like that for what felt like forever. When we finally stood up and I wiped the tears from my face, I knew we had a breakthrough. The way it happened may not have been pretty, but we both knew exactly where we stood in each other's lives. We were like family and I knew that this family would never desert me; that they would stand by me no matter what obstacles came my way.

Trish and I stayed outside together until the taxi arrived. Even though she told me to come back inside and wait for her to give me a ride, I couldn't. I was too exhausted – both physically and mentally – to face everyone in the house and I just wanted to go back to my room for the night. So I gave Trish a big hug, got in my taxi, and hoped that tomorrow would be a better day.

For the most part, the next day was better. Trish had set up a meeting for us to go to Suffolk Downs and meet with Christian Taja, the publicity director. He was going to give us a tour of the racetrack even though it was off season, and we were going to talk about maybe doing a book signing in the future.

When I first started talking to Christian, I tried to be as nice as I could. I asked if we could see the jocks' room and he hesitated. In that moment of hesitation, I felt all my anger and passion come back to me. I stood really close to him and practically demanded that he show us what we wanted to see. In the end, we got to take our tour, but I treated Christian unfairly and I knew it.

I was overwhelmed by my mental state and the fact that I hadn't been on a racetrack since I was handcuffed at Churchill Downs. That wasn't Christian's fault, but he was the one who had to hear about it. I never expected things to go the way they did. I loved Suffolk Downs. They were the first ones to let me wear an endorsement patch and they always welcomed me, even when I was acting unwelcome. The last thing I wanted was to have any problems with them. So when we left without talking about a book signing, I just hoped that we could work things out in the future and that our chances weren't completely blown.

After that situation, I felt a lot calmer and I enjoyed the rest of my trip. Trish and Sheryl took me to Anthony's Pier 4 to eat some genuine Maine lobster and I was delighted to order the biggest one in the place. With a 3.26 pound lobster and a cold bottle of beer by my side, I finally felt at ease.

The rest of the trip went by very quickly and I couldn't believe it was already time to go back to Louisiana. I said goodbye to Trish, Sheryl, and Anna and then prepared to go back home and start the phone calls and rejections all over again.

I wasn't looking forward to all the anger I knew those calls would bring, but if I wanted to cleanse my soul, I knew it was something I had to do. Never one to back down from a physical or mental battle, I was prepared to see this project through to the end – and this time I knew I wouldn't have to fight alone.

Chapter 34

In a final quote, George Orwell once penned the words, "Writing a book is a horrible, exhausting struggle, like a long bout of some painful illness. One would never undertake such a thing if one were not driven on by some demon whom one can neither resist nor understand." And if there's one thing I can say about me, it's that I was taken over by demons that I wanted to resist as much as I wanted to understand.

But as the book progressed further and I had to search my soul harder, I felt my inner demons taking me over completely. I was no longer myself. I was just an angry shell of the man I used to be and the exact opposite of the man I wanted to be.

Under that temperament, I went for a second trip to Boston to finalize some details for the book. I was excited to meet Tricia's father, Costas, because he was the man who made this book possible. He believed in his daughter and in my story enough that when Trish and I were unhappy with all the publishing companies' prospective deals, he gave us the money to self-publish. That was the kindest, most generous thing anybody had ever done for me and I was thrilled to meet the man who made it all possible.

Costas taught me all about Greek cooking and explained exactly why I should take a vacation to Greece. We hit it off right from the start and I felt blessed to be a part of Tricia's wonderful family.

Unfortunately, every blessing that I felt was attacked by yet another demon. On my second day in Massachusetts, Trish and I had an appointment to go for a photo shoot. I had spent the earlier part of the day with Trish, Mom, Costas, Sheryl and I focused so much of my energy on acting happy that I was completely drained. As Sheryl drove me back to my hotel, I knew that I couldn't possibly smile and act happy in front of a camera now. All I wanted was to go to sleep and I hoped everyone would understand. If Ididn't go to sleep, I knew I was going to have a major breakdown and that was the last thing I wanted.

When I got to my room, I was more than ready to escape the thoughts and feelings that were driving me into madness. I just wanted to fall into a deep oblivion and sleep my problems away. The trouble was that no matter what I did, I couldn't sleep. I tossed and turned this way and that, with all my thoughts swimming around my head like a lethal pool of sharks.

I sat up from my bed and took two Xanax to try to help me sleep. When that didn't work, I took two more. Then another two. By the end of the night, I took ten Xanax. As I lied in my bed, somewhere between being high and being tired, it occurred to me that I could have just caused myself serious harm. I was only supposed to take half to one pill a night and I had just taken ten. What if I overdosed? What if my attempts to fall into sweet sleep caused me to never wake up? With these fears on my mind and the faint sound of a TV newscaster announcing that actor Heath

Ledger died of an accidental overdose, I eventually drifted into an unconscious sleep.

The next day when I woke up, I was more scared than I could ever remember being. I couldn't make my eyes stay open and it was a struggle to keep my head up. When I got in the car, Trish and Sheryl were nervous for me. They could see the physical state I was in and when I started crying, they could also see my mental state. I told them what happened the night before and they were extremely worried. They thought I needed psychiatric help and I knew they were right. That night pushed me to the limit and I knew it was time to do something for myself.

The truth is I knew I needed help for a long time, but I always figured I would get it later. I didn't want to leave Kelli and the kids alone. I didn't want to abandon my farm. I didn't want to stop working on the book. One after another, excuses piled up in my head until I convinced myself that now wasn't the time to get help. But after my actions from the previous night, I was terrified and I knew it was really time.

Before I left Boston, I went out for one final meal with Trish, Anna, Costas, and Sheryl. We were going to go to one of Tricia's favorite restaurants, but after we won $500 on a scratch ticket – which was apparently the most exciting moment of Tricia's life – everyone decided to take me back to Kowloon Restaurant for more Chinese food and Scorpion Bowls. We had an excellent time there and the next day when I said goodbye to everyone at the airport, I promised that the next time I saw them, I would be a new man.

Once I got home, I was still enthusiastic about getting help, but it looked like help could not come that easily. I didn't have insurance, so if I wanted to get treatment, I would have to pay for it. Since that was something I certainly couldn't afford, I pushed the idea to the side for another month and spent my days lying on the couch and watching TV.

Then one day it was like an angel came down from Heaven, tapped me on the shoulder, and pointed me in the direction of my favorite horse owner, Barry Golden. I spoke to Barry on and off throughout the years, but I never told him how badly I was really doing. This time I couldn't contain my fears and troubles, so I told him the whole story. Barry was shocked to hear about everything that had happened to me. He didn't know the details about the Churchill Downs incident or about anything else that had happened to me. And since Barry knew a lot of things, it struck me that maybe other people didn't know, either.

As time went on, Barry and I spoke more frequently and he started talking with Trish and Anna, too. Like the rest of my family, Barry was truly concerned and he told me he wanted to help. He wanted me to be better and he was willing to pay for that to happen. So I received the second most generous offering in my lifetime just a few months after the first, and I accepted. I felt terrible allowing someone else to pay for my treatment, but I knew I needed it. I truly thought if I kept going down the path I was on that I would die, and as bad as things had been, I knew I wanted to live.

Kelli started searching for different inpatient treatment centers in Louisiana while Trish and Anna took care of the book. Anna created a beautiful MySpace profile for me and taught me how to use a computer. I imagine it's hard to teach someone how to use a computer by phone, but Anna managed to do it. And once I got the hang of it, MySpace turned into one of the great turning points of my life.

All of a sudden I was surrounded by people from my past who cared about me. I found Frankie Lovato and his wife Sandy, along with Nelson Medina and his wife Cindy, and it was like we had never left each other's sides. Then I found my childhood friend Mitzy and some wonderful fans I had never met. All of these people became like a security blanket and I suddenly knew I wasn't alone.

Around the same time, Trish started having much more success with her interviews. The first person she spoke to was Steve Sexton and he explained everything about the Churchill Downs incident the best he could. He was so helpful that he even gave her the names of some other people she should try to contact.

Then Trish spoke to people like Ken Patin, Jean Cruguet, Chris Rosier, Jose Martinez, Tony D'Amico, and Willie Martinez, all friends that I hadn't seen for years. She also spoke to my friend Gilda Libero from the New York racetracks, talked to my childhood buddy Kenny Desormeaux, and had Sheryl speak with my former agent Fred Aime. She even became friends with a man named John Maguire who runs a blog called The Race Is Not Always to the Swift. Though his first post about me wasn't the nicest thing I had ever read, Trish quickly discovered that John was a great guy who was truly interested in my story.

Before long, Trish didn't even have to try and track people down; they started coming to her. She received an e-mail from a woman named Jody Culmone Harvey who is the daughter of one of the greatest jockeys of all time, the late Joseph Culmone, and soon she started talking to Jody and her brother Joe. A horse owner named Rick Konwinski also contacted Trish and said it would be an honor to be interviewed, so Trish was more than happy to do so.

It took almost six months to get to this point, but it looked like things were finally falling into place and that this book was going to become a reality. I wasn't exiled from the industry like I thought; people just didn't know what happened to me nor did they realize that I had been here the whole time.

The unexpected influx of support affected me and made me really want to get help. I didn't just want to get better for me; I wanted to do it for my family, my friends, and everyone else in my life. I wanted to be the man I once was. I wanted to be *me* again.

So when I received word that I could finally get a bed at a facility, I did what the old Shane would have done. I went to church for a final blessing, kissed my family goodbye, and moved on to become the man I knew I could be.

Epilogue

I've said it before and I'll say it again: God has a plan for all of us. It took a lot of years and many more struggles for me to see God's plan, but now I know that he does have one and I know what I must do to carry it out.

God's plan was never for me to be miserable or sick or brokenhearted. He simply needed to bring me to the lowest of lows before he could get me to the highest of highs. And after one month at the Acadiana Addiction Center in Lafayette, Louisiana, I now know that the highest of highs has nothing to do with abused substances.

It took a long time for me to realize it, but I wasn't just mentally ill. I wasn't just tormented by a bad childhood or by the coming and going of friends and family. I was an alcoholic and addict. Before, I would have been ashamed to say such a thing. But now I'm proud to say I was an alcoholic and a drug addict, and I'm on the road to recovery.

For many years, I felt shackled; like my freedom was being stripped by everyone who held me on a leash, or rein. My father, the horse racing industry, my mental illness, my addictions … I always thought these things controlled me; that they kept me from being free. But now that I've freed myself from one problem, I see that my freedom was there all along. I just didn't know how to utilize it.

I've spent so much of my life being angry about things I couldn't control that I could hardly see the good that was in front of me. I lost sight of the way Kelli's eyes slowly close when she leans in to give me a kiss; of the way Shali smiles when she gabs on the phone with her girlfriends; of the way Saban's face strengthens during his lacrosse games; of the way my little Steiner giggles and squeals when she's truly happy.

I couldn't see the beauty of the ocean crashing against the shore or of snow glistening onto a streetlight. I couldn't see the happiness in just sitting with my family to eat a nice home-cooked dinner. I couldn't see the joy of going on vacation to meet friends and family from near and far.

Simply put, I couldn't see the joy of *life*.

Now that I'm clearheaded, I can see it all and the beauty is overwhelming. There is too much good in the world to only focus on the bad. A dark phase of my life is over and I can't wait to see all the brightness the future will bring.

I don't know exactly what the future holds for me, but I do know a couple of things. I no longer feel sorry for myself and for what I went through. I don't blame anybody for any of my problems. Sometimes things just happen.

My father may have been rotten to me, but I'm sure that wasn't his intention. I still don't feel ready to speak with him and I don't know if I ever will be. But I *do* know that I love him and that I thank him for giving me the strength I needed to get through the rest of my life.

I also realize that I can't blame anybody for what happened to me at Churchill Downs. For a long time, I thought it was everyone's fault and I thought the only cure was to find an answer for what happened. As it turns out, there *is* no answer. Steve Sexton can't explain it, the jockeys can't explain it, the owners and trainers can't explain it. Nobody knows what happened. And even if I go the rest of my life without knowing why things happened the way they did, that's okay. The point is that I got through it and I learned a lot of valuable lessons along the way.

The final realization I've made is that even though I received more than my fair share of grief over the fights I fought, it was all worth it. Horse racing is a magnificent sport and with a few adjustments, it could be perfect.

Now is the time for the industry to band together; for jockeys, trainers, owners, bug boys, valets, and everyone else to unite. If jockeys cannot get health insurance for themselves and their families, they should stand together and demand what they deserve. If jockeys are tired of heaving and sweating, they should address that problem together. If *anybody* wants to make changes in order for the whole industry to flourish, they have to work together.

Jockeys are a dying breed because most of them don't realize they could better themselves and the industry. Young boys don't want to be deprived of food, drink, and life; they want to be able to do what they love without risking their lives to do so. No more jockeys should have to *die* for the chance to ride.

Of course, plenty of people still want to ride and I hope they will pave the way for the next great generation of jockeys. Before I went to rehab, I had the pleasure of meeting one of those people. This boy knocked on my door and asked me if I would be his agent. When I patted him on the shoulder, I could feel the trash bags under his clothes that he wore to make himself sweat. And that's when I knew that even though I don't have it in me to be an agent, I *do* have it in me to make a difference.

When the dust from the writing process settles and I can resume a normal, healthy life, I know what I want to do with it. I want to open a school for would-be jockeys and teach them how to do things the right way. I want the future great jockeys from Louisiana to learn the best at my facility. I want these kids to learn how to make weight without starving themselves. If they cannot make weight at five percent body fat, then I'll have to tell them to leave. I don't want to hurt anyone's feelings or ruin anyone's future, but I also want to make sure these boys will *have* futures.

I cannot take on the industry by myself, nor do I want to. My riding days are over and now all I can hope for is that future riders will not have to endure all that I went through; all that *we* went through. If the industry and the public unite, changes can easily be made. Everyone needs to band together to make long-term, national changes, but I'll do everything I can to help people on an individual basis.

As I said before: Jockeys? They're a dying breed. But not if I can help it.

Acknowledgments

Shane Sellers and Tricia Psarreas would like to thank ...

... **Costas Psarreas** for making this book possible with his faith and generosity

... **Barry Golden** for being such a generous and wonderful influence

... **Anna Psarreas** for her beautiful book design and her outstanding contributions

... **Sheryl Maloney** for her dedicated time, effort, and support

... **Creative Projects** for their editing assistance

... **John T. Maguire** for spreading the word and believing in this book

... **Michael Ransom, Kristy Young, Theresa Robinson**, and **Kerri Gaither** from The Brighter Writer for their excellent contributions and undying support

... **Nick Papanikolaou** from Savage Dreams for his amazing website design

... **Renos Miliaris** from the band SEPTEMBER for his beautiful musical score

... **Michael Naimo** for capturing them so will in his pictures

... **Jean Cruguet, Ken Patin, Jose Martinez, Chris Rosier, Frankie Lovato, Nelson Medina**, and **Cindy Medina** for their support and jockey input

... **Fred Aime, Gilda Libero, Kenny Desormeaux, Rick Konwinski, Sandy Lovato, Jody Culmone Harvey**, and **Joseph Culmone** for sharing their knowledge and support

... **Tony D'Amico, Steve Sexton, Terry Meeks, Jerry Lasala**, and **Willie Martinez** for their kindness and assistance

... **Gulfstream Park, Arlington Park, Suffolk Downs,** and **Churchill Downs** for all of their assistance and support

... *And all of their family and friends who nourished them with their love and support, without which Freedom's Rein would still be nothing more than a wishful dream.*

Memorium

FREEDOM'S REIN is in memory of
Tricia Psarreas' late great-grandfather
"Pappou" Christy Yiakas,
A man who believed in all horse racing was
And all it could be again

This book is also in memory of
Chris Herrell and Emanuel Jose Sanchez
Who gave their lives to be a part of the
Sport of Kings

Book Club Guide

Please note that these questions contain spoilers, so it would be best to finish reading **Freedom's Rein** *before proceeding to these questions.*

1. The title *Freedom's Rein* represents all the freedoms that jockeys must give up to ride and how various people in the horse racing industry figuratively hold their lives by the reins. What types of freedom did you see stripped as you read the story and what would you do to regain your freedom in a similar situation?

2. *Freedom's Rein* delves deeply into the subject of eating disorders, conveying in detail exactly what jockeys must do to maintain their weights and the repercussions of following such a vicious cycle for so long. What do you suggest could be done to put less physical stress on jockeys' bodies and reduce the high occurrences of life-threatening eating disorders and the illnesses they can bring?

3. After reading about the arguments for and against changing the weight limits for jockeys, what is your stance? Do you think raising the weight limits would help the sport or hurt it? Do you think monitoring body fat percentages would be a better solution? Or do you think the weight system is fine the way it is?

4. *Freedom's Rein* contains many stories about how horses are treated in the racing industry. Clearly, many people in the industry love horses, but others are far more interested in money than in animals. What are your thoughts on what some of these animals go through? Where do you draw the line between necessity and abuse?

5. One of the main themes of *Freedom's Rein* is domestic abuse. Numerous studies show that domestic abuse, whether physical or emotional, can lead to several problems in one's life. What kind of role do you think Shane's upbringing played in the events that later occurred in his life?

6. As *Freedom's Rein* shows, Shane strongly believes that the horse racing industry could prosper if it were not for its lack of unity. Do you think a governing body would help the industry? Do you think jockeys will eventually band together to make such a change, or do you think they will stay quiet out of fear of being blackballed like Shane was for so long?

7. Throughout the course of his life, Shane has lost many people who he deeply loved. Some of these people turned their backs on him, but he also turned his back on others. What do you consider the main reason for Shane's frequent loneliness and the effect it had on his life?

8. Shane spent years battling his problems with drug and alcohol abuse. Many people would argue about whether drug and alcohol abuse fall into the categories of disease or habit. Do you believe that these addictions were inherited? Do you think they stemmed from Shane's high profile lifestyle as is the case with many athletes? Or do you think that some people are just more prone to drug and alcohol abuse (as either disease or habit) than others?

9. Perhaps the most prevalent theme in *Freedom's Rein* is that of love; love for one's family, love for one's friends, and love for one's self. Throughout the book, it becomes clear that Shane loves many people in many different ways. Do you think Shane was bettered or worsened because of all these types of love?

10. *Freedom's Rein* ends on an uplifting note of hope. Do you think the publication of this book will help Shane and his fellow jockeys achieve the changes they need? If not, what do you think could be done to improve the conditions of the horse racing industry for jockeys?

Coming Soon

FREEDOM'S REIN: THE COMPANION GUIDE

Now that you've read the story, it's time to read the facts. *Freedom's Rein: The Companion Guide* contains never before seen interviews, essays, and studies that bring the contents of *Freedom's Rein* to a whole new level.

Beginning with a foreword by Tricia Psarreas and ending with a section on how you can help make a difference, *Freedom's Rein: The Companion Guide* offers a shocking, behind-the-scenes look at what could bring the royal prestige back to the Sport of Kings.

To order your own copy of *Freedom's Rein: The Companion Guide,* please visit the Official Freedom's Rein Merchandise Shop.

www.FreedomsRein.com